SCOUTING OUT OF UNIFORM

HOW THE BOY SCOUT OATH & LAW CAN GUIDE YOU TO A SUCCESSFUL LIFE

BY

JOHN PATRICK HICKEY

To Chris – Thanks for learning to tie all the knots!

Published by Motivational Press, Inc.
1777 Aurora Road
Melbourne, Florida, 32935
www.MotivationalPress.com

Manufactured in the United States of America.

ISBN: 978-1-62865-531-5

CONTENTS

This book is dedicated to my brother Thomas E. Hickey, JR. a scout, marine, husband, father, brother, and to me, an all round Hero. You will never know the impact you have had on my life. I have learned so much from you and it has brought me to where I am today. You have my deepest love and gratitude.

I also dedicate this book to my grandson Dylan. You are my very favorite Scout. I am so proud of the Scout you are and the man you are becoming. Papa loves you so much.

THE SCOUT OATH

On my honor, I will do my best

To do my duty to God and my country

And to obey the Scout Law;

To help other people at all times;

To keep myself physically strong;

Mentally awake, and morally straight.

Taken from The Boy Scout Handbook 13th edition 2016

INTRODUCTION

HIKING THE ROAD TO SUCCESS

How the Boy Scout Oath & Law Can Guide You to a Successful Life

"Our aim is to produce healthy, happy, and helpful citizens; to eradicate the prevailing narrow self-interest; personal, political, sectarian and national, and to substitute for it a broader spirit of self-sacrifice and service in the cause of humanity and thus to develop mutual goodwill and cooperation not only within our own country, but abroad, between all countries."

Sir Robert Baden-Powell

1857-1941

Founder of The Boy Scouts

There are two dates in history that I would like to point out. First is January 24, 1908, which is the date that Sir Robert Baden-Powell, a well-known English war hero, founded the Boy Scout movement in England with the publication of his book, Scouting for Boys. The next date is February 8, 1910, which saw the founding of The Boy Scouts of America, here in the United States. And, as they say, the rest is history.

In the 108 years since the founding of the Boy Scouts of America (BSA) the movement has grown in masses of the numbers of boys, decreased to far lower numbers, has reached out to girls and has never stopped changing or improving. Another thing that has always been with the Scouting movement is controversy. Some battles they handled with skill and were better for them. Some, they failed miserably and have yet to recover from the damage.

> "To encourage physical, intellectual, emotional, social, spiritual and character growth in young people enabling them to take a constructive role in their local, national and international community."
>
> **Sir Robert Baden-Powell**
> **1857-1941**
> **Founder of The Boy Scouts**

The BSA has been loved, hated, praised and insulted. It has changed and transformed lives and though it may have faced its struggles, the country, indeed the world, has been better because of its existence. Scouts have shown us courage, kindness, good manners, Godly living and skills to be self-evident. Scouts have started great business enterprises, walked on the moon, been political leaders, doctors, lawyers, pastors, teachers, and inventors. Scouts have made a difference and we are all better because of them.

With all the changes that have taken place in the Scouting movement over the years, there is one thing that has remained the same, and that is the Scout Oath and Law. The Scout Oath and Law is the foundation of Scouting. It is what makes a Scout a Scout. It is so well known that even people who have never been in the Scouting program can recite the Scout Law.

The purpose of this book is to look at the Scout oath and Law from two different sets of eyes. First, to help those who are Scouts better understand and use the points of the Scout Law. They have been taught to memorize them, I want to help them live them. These Scouts will not be in the Scouting program all their lives. Some may get involved, like many have before you, with their own children when they are of the age to join Scouting. Many of the leaders in Scout Troops all over the country are those who went through Scout themselves. This why it is said, "Once a Scout, always a Scout." Some may move on to other things in their lives that do not include Scouting. Either way, they will all be living in the everyday world just like everyone else. This is to help them understand just how the Oath and Law will guide them along the way to a successful life.

The second is to help those who seek a successful life and to find a pathway that works. I call these people, success-minded people. I will explain more of how I define a success-minded person as you get into the book. But these are the types of people who believe there is a way to live successfully in all areas of life. I am not talking about money or position, but the ability to be your best at all you do and to live with honor, dignity, and knowing you make a difference.

I have been researching and writing about personal development for many years. I can honestly say I have found no better pattern for designing a life of integrity, hard work, and self-reliance than that of the Boy Scout Oath and Law. As you read through this volume you will understand that by following these simple 12 points, one can develop a life that impacts themselves, as well as the rest of the world.

Do not make the mistake of thinking that because you have never been a Scout this does not apply to you and your success in life. That is not the case. As you will learn, the Scout Oath and Law are timeless and work every time they are used. It also does not matter if you are male or female. It applies to everyone, no matter your race, economic status, where you live, what you do, and whatever you believe.

Please understand, this book and all that is in it, is my own opinions and does not reflect the thinking or the endorsement of the Boy Scouts of America. I in no way speak for them and I do not claim their support in this book. There is much where I fully agree and support the Scouting program. There are other things, and you will see them, where I have a different opinion than the Scouts. In short, this is not a BSA book.

My purpose here is not to sell you on the Scouting Program. If that happens and you encourage some young people in your life to join Scouting or you yourself become involved in Scouting due to something you read here, great. I do believe in the Scouting program and endorse it fully, but again, that is not my intent.

My desire is to show how the Scout Oath and Law can be used in our lives and help us be the best people we can be. I have found no better definition of good character than for us to strive to be trustworthy, loyal, helpful, friendly, courteous, kind, obedient, cheerful, thrifty, brave, clean, and reverent.

My prayer is you will read and benefit from this book. If we all do our best to become people of integrity, who work hard, care for others, and ourselves, we can make this world a better place. I want to start by telling you the five elements of personal success. These are, to be your best, love God, have good manners, discover the unknown and change your world.

CHAPTER 1

SCOUTING OUT OF UNIFORM

"Ideas are like stars: you will not succeed in touching them with your hands, but like the seafaring men on the ocean desert of water, you choose them as your guides and following them, you reach your destiny."

Carl Schurz

1829-1906

American Statesman

I first was exposed to Scouting, like many, when I was young. My mother was a Den Mother for all four of her sons. I loved Scouting. The camping and crafts we did were always fun. This was back in the late 50's and early 60's when Scouting was in its heyday. I don't remember too many of the boys in our suburban neighborhood who were not in Scouts. It was the one thing we all did together. I even remember our old Scout Master, Mr. McDonald who was a great example to us. He was always kind, helpful and made each of us feel we were important to the Troop. However, like many boys, when I got into my teen years I left Scouting and the good things it taught.

Fast forward about forty years or so, I had settled down, had a family and was working as a personal development coach as well as a pastor in a local church. I had become a Christian

> "The Scout Law is the foundation on which the whole of Scout training rests."
> **Sir Robert Baden-Powell**
> **1857-1941**
> **Founder of The Boy Scouts**

in 1974 and it made the greatest change in me. Some may say it caused me to stop all my bad and irresponsible habits, but I believe it helped me grow up. I was in my twenties and needed to take some responsibility for myself. Yes, knowing Jesus gave me the ability to do what was right, rather than continuing on my self-destructive path. I came to understand that there was a right and a wrong way to live. If I wanted to achieve something in life and be all I was created to be, then I needed to do what was good and right and stop the selfish and defiant life I had chosen for so many years.

In 2001, while on a treadmill for a stress test, my heart stopped. Luckily, I was in a hospital and help was there in seconds. I went from happily walking on the treadmill to waking up to someone pushing up and down on my chest. The doctors discovered that I had a damaged aortic valve in my heart. It was the same problem many athletes have, but I was no athlete, believe me, when they are actively playing football or basketball and suddenly fall over dead. The valve needed to be replaced with an artificial one, and soon. Within ten days after my heart stopped

I had heart surgery, which I am happy to say, was successful.

After the surgery, it took me months to recover and go back to work. At that time, they were still cutting my chest open to do work on my heart. My chest was cut open and they actually had to take my heart out. I was placed on a machine that kept my bold circulating while they removed the damaged valve and replaced it with an artificial one. I woke is the ICU on a respirator and tubes coming out all over me. Not an experience I would like to repeat. Today, it can be done with a small incision and the recovery can take only weeks. Modern medicine is a wonder.

Anyone who has had a lengthy recovery that they've gone through as a result of surgery knows it can become rather boring in just a short time. During that time, while looking for "something to do," I came across my old Boy Scout Handbook and decided to read it. Wow! It hit me like a brick. This stuff was good! It was like discovering all the things I have come to believe were taught to me many years ago, and I just forgot them somehow. The first thing to catch me was written in the introduction, it said, "As a Scout or Explorer, you are headed for new adventures and the purpose of this Handbook is to help you find it as you climb the trail to Eagle rank." I did not make it to Eagle rank, however I did find the adventure.

I believe that we all have a purpose in life and we can succeed at that purpose when we follow the principles of success. Success principles are like the laws of nature, they do not change and they do not grow old or die out. As I read the Scout Law, I realized they were the principles of success, listed and defined perfectly. These words were clear and simple enough that children, adults and anyone else in-between could understand them . We may change the wording depending on how we are presenting them, but the laws of success require that all become trustworthy, loyal, helpful, friendly, courteous, kind, obedient, cheerful, thrifty, brave, clean, and reverent.

I began to study how the Scout Law and the Laws of Success worked together in helping people be their best, love God, have good manners, discover the unknown and change the world (my mission). When my first grandson was old enough, I got him in Cub Scouts and became a leader myself. I never had a son, but I was greatly blessed with two daughters who have been my life. Together we have had many great adventures, but Scouting was just not one of them. In time, God gave me another great blessing, grandchildren! Ten of them to be exact. My oldest grandson was close by, so when he was old enough to go into Cub Scouts I made sure he did. It has been a great experience for the both of us.

As the year have gone by, my grandson is now a Boy Scout, has advanced in the ranks of Scouting and is now on his trail to becoming an Eagle Scout. e loves Scouting and is working hard to achieve his goal of becoming Eagle by the time he is 15 (a goal he has set for himself and I believe he will achieve). I am no longer a leader, but I am very involved in the Troop and in his Scouting experience. I serve on the Troop committee and am the Chaplain. I love Scouting and feel it is the best way for training young boys to make this world better.

This is where this book comes in. I am an author, trainer and personal development coach and I wanted to help people succeed by using the Scout Law. So why is it "out of uniform?" This is a personal account of my experience with the Scout Law and Oath and not sponsored by the Boy Scouts of America. It is something for everyone, young, old, male, female, Scouters, and non-Scouters. The Scout Law works for all who apply it to their lives.

I invite one and all to read this book and you will find that the principles here are things we all can and need to apply to our daily living. Who can say, "I don't need to be trustworthy, loyal, helpful, friendly?" The principles of the Scout Law are things we all must learn and apply every day to have a successful life. Those who live by these principles are what I call success-minded people. A success-minded person is one who is aware that success, in all areas of life, takes work, time and effort and they must be willing to put forth that work, time and effort to achieve it. I will talk more about success-minded people later.

Don't think that the Laws of Scouting are just for kids. Yes, iBut it is when we are adults these principles are the most important. t is important to teach these principles to our youth so they can grow and apply them when they are adults. We do not teach our children good manner or how to be honest, thinking that as adults they will no longer need the information. We adults, need to know and apply the principles of life just as much (if not more) as our children do. This book is not about the Scouting program, but about the Laws that make Scouting the wonderful and impactful organization it is.

The only way we will ever see improvement in our society is to see the people in it change for the better. Since you cannot change others, you have got to start with the one person you can change, yourself. Too many people wait for someone or something to change them and it never happens. To be a better person means that you are a responsible person. It is your decision to be all you can be and to add value to the world you live in. None of us are puppets who only do what a great puppeteer makes us do. Even God, your Creator, will not force you to do what is right. You must choose to live right. The great comedian, Carol Burnett said, "Only I can change my life. No one can do it for me." When you choose to become all you were created to be, not only will you be well on your way to a successful life, you will love the process.

THE SCOUTING PROGRAM AND SUCCESSFUL LIVING

For 107 years, the Boy Scouts of America have been teaching boys and young men how to be successful citizens and the best they can be in both their personal and professional life. Sadly, many people think these principles are only meant for boys and young men to earn badges and rewards, while they camp, hike and just have fun. Where the badges and rewards do play an important role in Scouting, the outdoor activities are also a vital part of the experience, the principles taught in the Scout Law and Oath are there to set a life pattern. These basic principles of success and better living will attract anyone who is looking to get the most out of their life and improve the world they live in.

The 12 key principles or points, known as The Scout Law, are simple to understand and easy to follow. It is something everyone we know can and should do to make our world a better place. People are looking for the keys to

"An individual step in character training is to put responsibility on the individual."

Sir Robert Baden-Powell
1857-1941
Founder of The Boy Scouts

be successful in life. They read books, go to seminars and attend classes, all of which are great things to do, but they sometimes miss the things that have been around for ages. You can read books dealing with the laws of success from Napoleon Hill to Tony Robbins and you will find the same principles in them all. Honesty, integrity, service to others and a positive attitude are just a few of the common attributes of successful people. They are also the attributes of the Scout. ou do not have to be a Boy Scout to appreciate and benefit from the Scout Law.

Here are the 12 things that we can learn about success from a Boy Scout.

1. THE IMPORTANCE OF BEING TRUSTWORTHY

No one likes dealing with a person who is dishonest. Even criminals expect those they work with to be honest with them. A trustworthy person is a person who you can believe and trust. They are a man or woman of their word and when they have a job to do, you know they will do it to the best of their ability. In business and in our personal lives, those who can be trusted are valued and sought after.

2. THE IMPORTANCE OF BEING LOYAL

Loyalty is a word that is not used much anymore and has lost some of its meaning. A loyal friend, companion or employee is one that is held on to. This is a quality that displays dependability; one who will not betray or misuse relationships in any way. A success-minded person will always show loyalty to which loyalty is due. Their honor and dedication are never in question.

3. THE IMPORTANCE OF BEING HELPFUL

In a world of "me first" and "this is not my job," the helpful person is treasured. Helpful people seek out ways they can assist others. They are success-minded people who think of others before they think of themselves. Helpfulness does not look for a reward or benefit from the service they offer. They do it because it is needed, no other reason. If you want to find success in this world, be helpful in every way you can. It will come back to you.

4. THE IMPORTANCE OF BEING FRIENDLY

Have you ever met a truly friendly person? They can light up a room and make everyone in it feel important. Being friendly is not something you are either born with or without, it is a choice you make every day. It starts with the knowledge that everyone you meet has something they can teach you. You are important to them as they are to you. Friendliness is easy to develop. A smile, a kind word and a desire to please all other people, are all that is needed and you too can make the world a better place.

5. THE IMPORTANCE OF BEING COURTEOUS

There was a time when everyone was expected to show good manners, but now, many think of manners as old fashion or unnecessary. Success-minded people understand that good manners will open more doors to you that education, wealth or talent ever will. Good manners are not just pleasing or knowing what fork to use and where to place your napkin. Good manners are simply treating others with respect and kindness. Good manners require us to think of others first and treat them as we wish to be treated by them.

6. THE IMPORTANCE OF BEING KIND

Mark Twain said, "Kindness is the language which the deaf can hear and the blind can see." Of all the principles of a successful life, nothing will bring you greater success in all areas and a deeper joy than kindness. Kindness is a quality we all desire to receive and should all desire to give. Kindness removes hurtful words and actions; it calms anger and can turn all things in your favor. Nothing speaks of a successful person like kindness.

7. THE IMPORTANCE OF BEING OBEDIENT

To be obedient does not mean you follow blindly and never question what you are told. Success-minded people understand that rules are there for a reason and that reason is not to break them. To be obedient, simply means you will follow the rules or the laws that you are given. We all have rules at work, at home, and in our communities. If a rule or law is unfair, unnecessary or immoral, the obedient person does what is needed to change that rule or law in an orderly and peaceful manner.

8. THE IMPORTANCE OF BEING CHEERFUL

If you have two people, who have the same qualifications for a job and the same level of ability, but one is grumpy and complains all the time and the other is cheerful and positive, who will you hire? The positive, cheerful person gets the job every time. Cheerfulness, like friendliness, is a choice we make, not a talent we are born with. No one likes to be around an unpleasant grump. Keep positive and cheerful and not only will others want you around, but you will feel better as well.

9. THE IMPORTANCE OF BEING THRIFTY

To be thrifty is more than just the ability to save money and not over spend. Thrifty people have a respect for property, their own and that of others. They know that waste is never a good thing and they do their best to care for what they have and to respect the use of what belongs to others. Whether at work, home or out in the community, a thrifty person will not destroy things, vandalize or leave their trash where it does not belong.

10. THE IMPORTANCE OF BEING BRAVE

The world is in great need for those who are brave. The brave person will stand for what they know is right, no matter who or what tells them differently. It takes a brave person to believe there is right and wrong in this world. That good and evil do exist and the brave person will always stand for the good and right. Compromise is not part of the life of the brave. They know at times they will stand alone, but they will stand all the same. These are the people who will do what is right, just because it is the right thing to do.

11. THE IMPORTANCE OF BEING CLEAN

Success-minded people know there is more to being clean than what you do with soap and water. They know how they dress matters. You will not achieve the respect or success you desire if you go around looking like you just rolled out from under a rock. There is a reason why sloppy people, in their dress and their lives, do not find success. If you don't care about you, how can you care about anything else?

12. THE IMPORTANCE OF BEING REVERENT

Here is where people tend to feel that someone is stepping on their toes. Many do not like it when others talk to them about spiritual things. Success-minded people know that spiritual awareness is an important part of who we are as people. The person who understands reverence can respect the beliefs, not only in others, but also in themselves. They know they can allow others to believe as they wish and see how their beliefs will affect what they do. They also are willing to honor their own beliefs and not do things contrary to them.

THE SCOUT LAW AND EVERYDAY PEOPLE

As a boy, James Stephen, "Steve" Fossett (1944-2007) found Scouting to be his key to a life of adventure. The son of an Eagle Scout, Fossett received the highest rank in Boy Scouts, that of Eagle, at the age of 13. He loved the adventure and excitement   Scouting

"The heroes of the wild, the frontiersmen and explorers, the rovers of the sea, the airmen of the clouds are Pied Pipers of the boys."
Sir Robert Baden-Powell
1857-1941
Founder of The Boy Scouts

offered him. Living in California, he climbed mountains, hiked desert trails and spent as much time as he could camping and being outdoors.

The result of this passion for Scouting developed two main areas in Steve Fossett's life. One was a highly successful businessman, and the other was becoming one of the greatest explorers and adventures of modern times. Being an explorer was not what he did; it was who Steve Fossett was.

In business, Steve Fossett understood the principles he learned about hard work, persistence and making wise decisions. After receiving his MBA from Olin School of Business at Washington University in St. Louis, Missouri, Fossett worked for several companies including IBM, Deloitte and Touché and Marshall Field. He later discovered he had a real passion and talent for finances. "For the first five years of my business career," Fossett said, "I was distracted by being in computer systems, and then I become interested in financial markets. That's where I thrived."

As the years went on, Fossett buildt a very successful business, allowing him to accumulate a great fortune. However, money and success were never really the driving force behind Steve Fossett. It was always the challenge and the chance to do the impossible. This drive would lead him to his true passion, adventure.

From his early days in Scouting and throughout his life, Steve Fossett never saw a challenge too big or impossible. In fact, the more impossible a challenge was, the more determined Fossett was to achieve it. This is why he broke and held (some to this day) records in sailing, aviation, and climbing. He was the first person to fly nonstop around the world in a balloon. Five times he went nonstop around the earth by balloon, boat and a fixed wing aircraft.

So, what was the foundation that Fossett would later say gave him the ability to achieve these great feats in life? "As a Scout," Fossett said, "I learned how to set goals and achieve them. Being a Scout also taught me leadership at a young age when there are few opportunities to be a leader. Scouting values have remained with me throughout my life, in my business career and now as I take on new challenges." Steve Fossett's commitment and involvement in the Boy Scouts did not diminish through the years. He took on many leadership roles, including becoming a member of the BSA National Executive Board and the President of the National Eagle Scout Association in 2007 till his death later that year.

Many Scouts look up to Steve Fossett as the example of all Scouting can be. Fossett was not born a super hero or given advantages that others lacked. He was an average middle-class boy who found, in Scouting, the opportunity to become all he was created to be. It was the lessons he learned in Scouting, the Scout Law and Oath that gave him direction and knowledge to go on and achieve real greatness.

These principles are available to us all if we are open and willing to learn. I am amazed at how quickly people will dismiss the ideas in the Scout Law, simply because they have some misconceived idea of what Scout is or should be.

Scouting has produced many great leaders and adventures as well as businessmen, statesmen, military leaders and the most successful people in about every field of endeavor. We have had Scouts as business leaders, entertainers, and top educators and out of the 12 astronauts that walked on the moon, 11 were Scouts. We have even had several elected as President of the United States.

Robert Gates, the former Secretary of Defense, who also served as the 35th President of the BSA from 2014-2016 and is an Eagle Scout, also claims that his experience in Scout greatly affected his life and career. "I don't think there is an organization in the world," Secretary Gates said, "certainly not in the United States, that better prepares young men for leadership in this country than the Boy Scouts of America – in teaching leadership skills, in teaching values, in teaching importance of standing up for what's right."

The 46th United States Secretary of State, Rex Tillerson, has also proudly served the Boy Scouts of America as their 33rd President. Secretary Tillerson has spent most of his life in Scouting, starting as a Cub Scout and taking it all the way to his Eagle rank. He once said, "I think the highlight of my youth and adolescent years were my achievements in Scouting." His close friend, Ray L. Hunt said to the Dallas Morning News, "To understand Rex Tillerson, you need to understand Scouting."

Secretary Tillerson has shown he is a tireless worker who knows how to achieve his goals in life. Successful businessman, he has spent most of his career with the same company. He started as an engineer with Exon-Mobil in 1975 and by 2006 he was the CEO of the company. Explaining his career, Secretary Tillerson said, "Throughout my life and career, I have continually been impressed with the importance of integrity – whether it was growing up as a Boy Scout, working in one of my first jobs as a university janitor, or being a leader in a Fortune 500 company."

The principles and skills taught in the Scouting program are not things that young people memorize only to forget when they are adults. They are not passing lessons that have no use in adult life. The principles taught in the Scout Law and Oath are ones that will guide a person throughout their whole life. These principles of integrity, loyalty, respect, and kindness (provided they are followed) can take any person, man or woman, Scout or non-Scout, and keep them on a road to success.

Former Major League Baseball player, manager, and Hall of Famer, Tommy Lasorda shared this, "I still remember the entire Boy Scout motto. I don't remember the serial number of my gun in the army. I don't remember my locker in school. But I remember that Boy Scout Code." I know not everyone who has been a Scout has gone on to follow the Boy Scout Law, but I can promise you they have not forgotten it.

"The Boy Scouts of America will prepare every eligible youth in America to become a responsible, participating citizen and leader who is guided by the Scout Oath and Scout Law."

Vision Statement of the Boy Scouts of America

BEING OUT OF UNIFORM

The concept of "being out of uniform" has two meanings. The first is to make it clear that the content here, although consistent with the Boy Scout Law and Oath, does not have the official backing of The Boy Scouts of America.

> "We never fail when we try to do our duty, we always fail when we neglect to do it."
> **Sir Robert Baden-Powell**
> **1857-1941**
> **Founder of The Boy Scouts**

Personally, I may be involved in Scouting and am a Scout myself, but I do not speak for the BSA. Thus, I am out of uniform.

Part of the official policy of the BSA concerning the use of the uniform, according to Burgin Hardin is the BSA's licensing and contracts attorney, is as follows..

"Most everyone is familiar with the BSA's famous trademarks, such as the fleur-de-lis and the phrase "Eagle Scout." But there are many other symbols and devices that represent the BSA and its programs that are protected by law.

"For instance, in addition to the individual badges and emblems on a Boy Scout uniform, the uniform as a whole is protectable under U.S. trademark law. BSA's intellectual property rights in its uniforms — Boy Scout, Cub Scout, and Venturing — derive from the uniforms' distinctive combination of colors and styles. Over time, the public has come to recognize those combinations as symbols of the Boy Scouts of America. Thus, when a member does his or her uniform, they are, quite literally, a walking symbol of the BSA." (From the article: How the BSA views unauthorized use of the Scout uniform by non-Scouts, by Bryan Wendell, January 14, 2015)

Yes, I know I am talking about the Scout Law and Oath and not wearing the uniform, but I respect all things Scouting and consider these principles just as much a part of the Scouting program as the uniform.

The second reason for the term, "out of uniform" is to help the reader understand the principles and statements in this book are for all people, Scouters, on-scooters, men, women, young and old alike. They are not just principles and lessons designed for those in Scouts. The Scout Law and Oath has something to teach all who wish to live a fully successful life. You do not have to be in the uniform of a Boy Scout to live like one.

Well-known author and speaker, Zig Ziglar, once said, "Following the Scout Law sounds like a game plan that would give us all a better chance for success in life – and I mean every area of life." Mr. Ziglar believed and often taught that success was not just about position, wealth, or fame. To be truly successful in life, you needed to have all areas of life in the right place. Along with your work and career, it includes your personal life, your relationships with family and friends and your spiritual life.

When we talk about success, we tend to think in terms of wealth and achievement. There is nothing wrong with great achievements or even the accumulation of wealth. However, success, true success, does not stop there. You can achieve all your dreams and have more money than most small countries and still be a failure. Success means little if your bank account is big but your family is falling apart. Spending a fortune is no fun if that spending is for lawyers who need to cover your dishonest or criminal practices. It is as the Bible says, "What profits a man if he gains the whole world and loses his own soul."

The success principles taught in the Scout Law and Oath are those of personal development. They are designed to build good character and be a true moral compass. When followed, they will lead you to great achievements and success in all you do. However, that success will come from you being the best person you can be. Always remember that good character is not the result of success, it is the cause of it.

Success-minded people are those who believe their behavior and character matters most in life. They know if they are to achieve their dreams and be the best at all they do, they must first develop as a person. This personal development is something that does not stop once a success in some field is achieved. Success-minded people work on their own development as long as they have the breath to live another day.

CHAPTER 2

THE SUCCESS-MINDED PERSON

"Associate with well-mannered persons and your manners will improve. Run around with decent folk and your own decent instincts will be strengthened."

Stanley Walker

1908-1993

British Athlete

To help define just what a success-minded person is and how that relates to the Scout Law, I have written what I believe to be the 12 characteristics of a success-minded person. By no means is this the final definition and last word on character development, but it is a good start. As you go through this list, note what areas you are strong in and where you may need some improvement. We will be visiting these characteristics through this book and each will be defined in much more detail. Right now, this list is to help you see the qualities of a success-minded person and allow you to take a personal inventory of your own state.

12 CHARACTERISTICS OF A SUCCESS-MINDED PERSON

HONORABLE

A Success-Minded Person is someone who can always be trusted. They do not lie, cheat or behave in a dishonest manner. They understand their honor is the most precious quality they hold and protect it at all cost.

FAITHFUL

A Success-Minded Person is loyal to their employer and workplace, co-workers, friends, church, Pastor, and organizations they are affiliated with. Lastly, and perhaps most of all, to their God, spouse, family, and country.

"A Scout is active in doing good, not passive in being good."

Sir Robert Baden-Powell
1857-1941
Founder of The Boy Scouts

USEFUL

A Success-Minded Person must be prepared to help others whenever needed. This can be to help those who facing some kind of difficulty or just a simple act of kindness The helpful person is one who looks for a way they can do something helpful for those around them.

COMPANIONABLE

A Success-Minded Person is a friend to everyone. They will always be ready with a smile and an encouraging word. They value their friends and make sure to show it in any way they can.

RESPECTFUL

A Success-Minded Person is polite to all, understands and practices good manners. They never fail to say, "please & thank you." They believe in and hold on to the Golden Rule of doing to others as they want others to do for them. To the success-minded person, good manners are a way of life.

KIND

A Success-Minded Person knows that kindness is the best way to touch others and make a better life. They are aware of the feeling of others and avoid saying hurtful things, whether it is in a critical comment, a remark made in anger or an unkind joke.

LAW-ABIDING

The Success-Minded Person obeys the law. They will follow the policies and rules in the workplace and strive to do beyond what is expected of them. They help shape the policies of the workplace and the laws of the community by being involved in the organizational process.

POSITIVE

A Success-Minded Person has a positive attitude and is optimistic about all things. They can always be depended on for encouragement, a positive perspective, and creative thinking. They smile at and speak kindly to all they meet.

FRUGAL

A Success-Minded Person saves their money so they may pay their own way in life. They do not look to other people or the government to care for them or meet their needs. A Success-Minded Person is generous to those in need, tithes to the church, and is helpful to worthy causes. They take care of their possessions, do not waste their resources and respect the property of other people, or that of their community.

COURAGEOUS

A Success-Minded Person has the courage to face daily challenges despite fear, and stand up for what is right and Godly against the coaxing of friends or the jeers or threats of enemies. They have the courage to do what is right just because it is the right thing to do.

ORDERLY

A Success-Minded Person keeps clean in body, thought, stands for clean speech, clean sports, clean habits, and travels with a clean crowd. They are aware of what they watch, read and listen to always.

DEVOUT

A Success-Minded Person is respectful toward God and His commandments. They have a personal relationship with Jesus Christ and that relationship directs their life. They are active in service to the church and community. They will respect the convictions of others in matters of custom and religion. However, they will always be ready to give an account of the hope that is within them.

ON MY HONOR

Most everyone understands and uses the term, "Scout's Honor." It is usually said when you are either promising to do something or claiming to be telling the truth. If a person is making a promise and wants to stress the fact that they really do mean what they are saying, they put up three fingers, in the Scout salute and say, "Scout's Honor, I will do it."

Why has this practice been around for so long? I remember people using it when I was a boy, many years ago. I still see it used and see that most people, young and old, know right away what it means. This is because the honor of the Scout is seen to be a promise that will not be broken. The honor of the Scout means something.

There are still many institutions in this country, which hold fast to the importance of honor. The U.S. military is such an organization. Honor is not just a word of concept that looks good on paper. My brother, to whom this book was dedicated is a career Marine. When I was young, and I must say, very foolish, I did not appreciate who he was or what he did for our country, his family or for me personally. As I grew up, I came to understand what it meant to me a person of honor. Not one who is boisterous and pushy, but one who believed in what was right and stood for it. One also, who was just as ready to forgive as he was to stand against. Today, when I think of a man of honor, he holds the first place in my mind.

In his excellent book, West Point Leadership Lessons, business consultant, and former West Point Class President, Scott Snair talks much about the honor that is held in high regard at the world famous, West Point Military Academy, in West Point, NY. In it, he tells of a former superintendent of the academy, Colonel Sylvanus Thayer, who was known as "The Father of Military Academy." It was Colonel Thayer who established what is known as the Code of Honor in the 1800's. That code reads.

> "The Code of the Knight is still the code of the gentleman today."
> **Sir Robert Baden-Powell**
> **1857-1941**
> **Founder of The Boy Scouts**

"A Cadet will not lie, cheat, steal, or tolerate those who do."

Snair said, "The code is as powerful as it is simple. This straightforward, unwavering nature lays the groundwork of trust and dependability upon which all good, productive things can be built." The importance of this lesson is sometimes lost in a society that feels compromise is better than standing for what is honest, good and right. Scott Snair calls this commitment to honor, the "harder right." He says, "West Point teaches this concept as choosing 'the harder right over the easier wrong,' meaning people frequently do not respond well to actions of pure integrity around them."

We have seen this with Scouting for many years. It is as common to use the term, "Scout's Honor" when making a promise, as to call someone a "Boy Scout" when they refuse to do what is wrong or to compromise their values. Both terms by-the-way, are seen as a badge of honor for the Scout. It is always better to be seen as the one to make a promise they will keep and be uncompromising when it comes to honesty and right behavior.

The start of the Scout Oath is, "On my honor." That is not just a simple statement. Scouts understand you are making a commitment, a sacred promise, to do their duty. As you read over this oath you are reminded that this goes far deeper than just promising to behave and do what is right. The Scout is taught that they are committing themselves to a way of life that cannot be compromised or misinterpreted.

It clearly states in the Scout Handbook, "On My Honor...Honor is the core of who you are – your honesty, your integrity, your reputation, the way you treat others, and how you act when no one is looking. By giving your word at the outset of the Scout Oath, you are promising to be guided by its ideals."

The way to live a successful life in all areas is to begin by being a person of honor. No one can live truly successfully and not be trusted by others, or by themselves. Honor is the standard that all people should be striving for at all times. There is no better way of life and, to the man or woman who wishes to transform their world, a life of honor is their only option. Less than honor is just not acceptable.

This promise of honor to do one's duty is defined in the Scout Law. In the 12 points of the Scout Law, a person can find the guidelines for living a successful and happy life. Maybe not an easy life, but as Scott Snair said, "We choose to live the harder right to the easier wrong."

CHAPTER 3

BEING HONORABLE

(A Scout is Trustworthy)

"Train em'. Trust em'. And let them lead."

William Hillcourt

1900-1992

Author of the Scoutmaster's Handbook

"A Scout is trustworthy. A Scout tells the truth. He is honest, and he keeps his promise. People can depend on him."

The Boy Scout Handbook

13th Edition

Honor and trustworthiness are one and the same. Just as honor goes far deeper than just doing what is right, so trustworthiness is more than people being able to trust you. Honor is not what a person does it is who they are. Honorable people live with the understanding that truth, dependability, trust, and sacrifice are present in both their public and private life. Honor demands that we truly walk the talk. People know that a person of honor will follow through on their promises and even when they are alone, they will not compromise or betray that trust.

I am tempted to add here the classic saying, "No one is perfect." That is a true statement. No one is perfect and the person of honor fully understands that. However, here is where they may differ from some. Too often we use the saying, "No one is perfect" as an excuse for our failings. If no one is perfect then we cannot expect people to be perfect. We can compromise our principles, give into our fleshly desires or do what we know is wrong, and use our imperfection to cover it up.

"Trust should be the basis for all moral training."
Sir Robert Baden-Powell
1857-1941
Founder of The Boy Scouts

The person of honor sees and understands they will fail in some way from time to time, but they do not accept that as an excuse or even a possibility. Honor holds us to the highest standards. People of honor know that to do what is right and good is a deliberate act and one that does not come naturally. It is a common belief that most people are basically good. The difficult fact to accept is that most of us, by nature, are selfish. We all tend to think of ourselves first. The good comes when we are willing to put aside out selfish interests and think of others. That, however, is a deliberate act that we choose to do. Fortunately, many people do make that choice and think of others before themselves.

However, if you look at the world you live in, it does not take much to see that selfishness still holds its power over people. .

I am not saying humanity is hopeless and we are all doomed to do what is evil and bad. In spite of our propensity to do wrong and rebel, we humans are also given the greatest power in the universe, the ability to choose. We all have the ability to choose to do what is right and good. We choose to give into our selfishness or we choose to do what is right. You are never without the ability to choose – never.

As I said, the person of honor is just someone who has purposely and deliberately chosen to be honest, truthful and selfless. They are no different from anyone else in that, they could if they chose to, do wrong just as easy as they do good. Truth is it is far easier to do what is wrong and selfish, than it is to do what is good, right and selfless. In the words of author and speaker, Corrie ten Boom (1892-1983), "Any dead fish can swim downstream."

When a Scout is taught to be trustworthy, he is not learning how not to get caught. He knows this is more than the first point of the Scout Law, it is the foundation of character. If you cannot be trustworthy, you will find it impossible to be loyal, helpful, friendly, courteous, kind, obedient, cheerful, thrifty, brave, clean and reverent.

You might ask, "How does not being trustworthy effect being friendly, or helpful or even kind? How close of a friend can you be if people cannot trust you? Do you ask for help from someone who you cannot depend on? How many selfish people do you know who are truly kind?

One of the keys to understanding the Scout Law is every point is dependent on the others. These twelve points of the Scout Law fit together in building one character. They are designed to help the whole person, not just one aspect of that person. Honor is an outcome of true character, it does not exist in one or two good points.

On May 2, 2017, the world lost a great man of honor. Lieutenant Colonel Leo K. Thorsness of the United States Air force and Medal of

Honor recipient entered the presence of his Lord at the age of 85. Lt. Col. Thorsness was a man of honor, bravery, and sacrifice. As an Air Force pilot during the Vietnam War, his assignment was to discover and destroy North Vietnamese surface-to-air missile sites. He bravely uses himself as a target to expose their positions for the American troops to destroy.

Time and time again, Lt. Col. Thorsness placed himself in danger to save the lives of his fellow soldiers and fight the enemy. He was the only Medal of Honor recipient credited with an aerial victory in the Vietnam War. Lt. Col. Thorsness saw this as his duty as an American soldier.

On April 30, 1967, Lt. Col. Thorsness was shot down over North Vietnam and captured. He spent six years as a prisoner of war in the infamous, Hanoi Hilton, prison camp. He endured torture, starvation, and isolation, until his release in 1973. Lt. Col. Thorsness would later give the credit to his survival and leadership qualities to the skills he learned as a Boy Scout.

"Many people know that Scouts are trained in first aid." he said in an article for Veterans Today, March 28, 2011, "But do you know what else Scouts are trained in? Courage. And leadership. And service. I must say this with some humility, because I, myself, am an Eagle Scout."

Lt. Col. Thorsness also received the Distinguished Eagle Scout Award from the BSA. He is one of nine Scouts who received the award as well as the Medal of Honor. Scouts have a rich history of building men of courage and honor, who go above and beyond what is expected of them. Lt. Col. Thorsness said, "The Boy Scouts of America not only prepares young people to act heroically and courageously in times of crisis, but it also prepares young people for life."

You do not have to be at war or suffer great tragedy to be a person of honor. Never make the mistake of thinking the situation makes a person of honor. The ability to show courage in a time of crisis or the strength to stand when many would cower away is developed in the person, not outside them. The difficulties of life will show honor in a person, it does not create it. A person is honorable; some outside event does not make them honorable.

As we develop into a success-minded person, we must ask ourselves this question, "Am I an honorable person?" The answer is not meant to produce guilt or pride; it is to help us on our path to success in life. If we lack in some area, we can always change that and do what is necessary to become the person we desire to be. If you are strong in some area, good, use it to help you become stronger in other areas as well. It is important success-minded people realize that to be a person of character and honor is not just for difficult and straining times. In fact, success is the greater judge of true character. As Former President, Abraham Lincoln (1809-1865) said, "Nearly all men can stand adversity, but if you want to test a man's character, give him power."

Honor, or trustworthiness, is as much for ourselves as for others. You must be honest with yourself before you can be truly honest with others. Honest people know they will always have room to improve. That is not a

> "The more responsibility the Scoutmaster gives his patrol leaders, the more they will respond."
> **Sir Robert Baden-Powell**
> **1857-1941**
> **Founder of The Boy Scouts**

short fall, it is the way life works. Back to the saying, "No one is perfect." Where it is not an excuse to fail, it is a reason to advance. You will never reach the point where honor and truthfulness are natural to you. It will always be a deliberate act. The question is, are you willing to pursue that place of honor and never stop striving for perfection? Coach Vince Lombardi (1913-1970) said, "Perfection is not attainable, but if we chase perfection we can catch excellence."

CAN YOU BE TRUSTED?

I have seen it repeatedly. The leader, employer, Scout Leader or parent who gives a task to someone and then hovers over them, "making sure they do it right." They micro-manage it so much that the person doing the job loses all interest in doing it right; they just want to be done. Then, the leader, employer, Scout Leader or parent complain, they cannot understand why their worker or child has no interest in doing what they are given to do.

Here is a fact of life: No one likes to be micro-managed - NO ONE! When someone is watching over your shoulder all the time it gives you the message that you are not trusted. It says the person in charge thinks you are incompetent and unable to do the work you are given. This, more than any problem a person may face, sucks the life out of those expected to do the task. The results are, the person in charge gets exactly what they are expecting, failure.

The thing with being trustworthy is it has to come from both sides. If the person who desires to show they are trustworthy is always met with distrust or criticism for everything they are trying to do, then they lose the desire to complete the task. This is especially true with young people, I have seen it over and over again, a young person who wishes to prove they not only can be trusted to do a job, but they want to do it well. They are faced with a leader, parent or teacher who, from the start, tells them they cannot be trusted and that they will mess things up. They feel, why bother? And they are right.

Here are some rules that all leaders must follow to get the best out of others.

LEAVE THEM ALONE

When you give a job to be done or a task to manage to someone, allow them the freedom to be responsible. Leave them alone! Allowing them to do the task without your oversight will show that you trust them. We all want to be trusted and have someone believe the best of us. The person who feels trusted to do a good job will give their best. We want to please those who honor us. We do not give our best to those who do not believe we have the best to give. Author, Earnest Hemingway (1899-1961) said, "The best way to find out if you can trust somebody is to trust them."

YOU GET WHAT YOU EXPECT

There is an old saying, "Want a bad kid, tell them they are a bad kid." People will give us just what we expect of them. Those who micro-manage tell others they expect them to do a poor job or to fail. They may not say so in direct words, but that is the clear and direct message they give. When trust is given, you tell others that you believe in them. You allow them the power to be the best they can be and with that, they will give back just what you expect - excellence.

SEEK RESULTS, NOT POWER

Let's face it, most people who micro-manage do not want good results, they want control. For those who understand that success comes from a team working together, not from who is in control, they will allow others to do it their way. We are all different and have different styles of learning and achieving. When giving a task to be done, be clear on the results you want, not on the steps to do it. Allow those doing the task to do it their way, if the needed results are achieved, there is no need to worry about the methods.

Success-minded people know the best way to get excellence from another person is to expect it and allow it. Let those you are working with, no matter on what level, do their best and you will have the success you seek.

In Scouting, leaders understand that it is designed to be "boy lead." That means that the adult is there to help answer questions, give guidance and to be a support, they are not there to run the show. I have seen this is a struggle for both the adults as well as the scouts. The adults are used to running the show. Some feel responsible for things to run well and they help the Scouts avoid failure, others just do not want to deal with things taking time. They want it done so they just do it.

The problem is on the Scout's side as well. Scouts are used to the adults running the show. They fear failure and that if they goof up, they will be scolded or punished. Besides, it is easier to just let the adults do things, rather than deal with them.

The best way, of course, is to allow the Scout to do it "their way," and unless needed, stay out of it. Explain what needs to be done, give them some direction, but not instructions, and let them know that if they fail, it is okay and they can try again. The best way to allow them to earn your trust is to freely give it to them, and let them know it.

TRUTH IS MORE THAN NOT LYING

Many years ago, I worked as a professional storyteller. People often asked me what was the difference between a storyteller and a professional storyteller. "It means," I would answer, "I get paid for it." I loved to tell people storytellers and politicians have much in common. We both tell a lot of fiction. It is expected that both storytellers and politicians tell lies. The difference is storytellers admit it and politicians try to make you believe they are telling the truth.

Storytelling is a grand tradition and one people enjoy. The tagline on my business card read: Everyone Loves a Good Story, and they do. Lying, on the other hand, may be a tradition, but people do not enjoy it at all. People do not like feeling deceived. When we know that we have been lied to, we lose trust in the people.

America has been through a very difficult time when it comes to our leaders and the truth. The American people do not feel they can believe anyone anymore, not the media, not our

> "Correcting bad habits cannot be done by forbidding or punishment."
> **Sir Robert Baden-Powell**
> **1857-1941**
> **Founder of The Boy Scouts**

leaders in government and sadly, not even each other. This lack of trust leads to a detrition of our society as a whole. As America's 31st President

Herbert Hoover (1874-1964) once observed, "When there is a lack of honor in government, the morals of the whole people are poisoned."

Some people think if they do not openly tell a lie, it is the same as telling the truth. However, a lie can be what we do not say as well as what we say. When we know the truth about a matter and do not say that truth, it is the same as if we straight out lied about it. Honest people do not ignore the truth, they do something about it. Our actions can lie louder than any words we may speak – or not speak. As American humorist and author, Mark Twain (1835-1910) use to say, "Action speaks louder than words, but not nearly as often."

For example, if someone believes you did something for them that you really did not do, but you do not correct them, it is still a lie. I remember a young man in youth group at a church I was pastoring at, he was asked by the youth leader to clean up a room before a meeting. The young man then told a friend to take care of the room and the friend did. When the youth leader saw the fine job done on the room he openly thanked the young man and even used him as an example to the other youth of someone who could be depended upon. The young man never corrected the leader and allowed him to believe he did the job. When confronted about this by someone who knew the truth, the young man said he did not lie about it; he just did not correct the leader's mistake. "After all," the young man said, "I was asked to see the room was clean, he never asked me to do it myself."

I know many people will think this makes sense. He did see that the room was clean. It is true that if you are asked to do a task, it may not mean that you have to actually do it. You just need to see that it gets done. The lie came in when the young man allowed the leader to think he actually did the job himself. He could have said, "I did not actually clean it myself, I asked so-and-so to do it and they did a great job." But, as we know, that is not what happened.

Life is full of these types of situations. You may often find that someone has mistaken a good deed to be done by you and you know full well who really did it. Honor is the ability to correct this misunderstanding right away and to give full credit to the one who deserves it. I know these mistakes can seem to be to your advantage, and some may call them a "blessing." However, a lie, no matter how or why it is told, is never to your advantage.

It is never enough to just tell the truth, you must live the truth. A person of honor is one who can be depended upon to always be honest and truthful. One that does not take credit for what they have not done and will not purposely give a false impression of their actions. These are people who understand that character is more important than being recognized.

It is often easy to be honest about yourself when you are in the wrong and things do not go your way. It is harder to be honest when things are in your favor and can help you advance in life. The 16th U.S. President, Abraham Lincoln (1809-1865) had this in mind when he said, "Nearly all men can stand adversity, but if you want to test a man's character, give him power."

The desire to get ahead and take advantage of all opportunities that come your way, whether they are real or false, has been the destruction of many people. In teaching young people the value of being trustworthy, the Scouting program is preparing them for the challenges that can come from the world they live in. Telling the truth, in word or action, is one of the most important lessons we can learn. As an author, Bo Bennett states, "For every good reason there is to lie, there is a better reason, to tell the truth."

Here is something that is very important to remember. How you handle the truth will affect everything in your life. If you can be trusted to tell the truth, not only in your words, but also in your actions, people will trust you with almost anything. It affects the way you work, play, worship and serve others. You will find doors open to you that might otherwise be closed. You will find opportunities for growth and development that you may not have had a chance at before. Relationships will strengthen and build. There is no part of your life that will not be affected by trustworthy behavior.

Think about this in your own life. Do you trust just anyone with your secrets, your possessions or your future? I am sure the answer is no. You will trust what is dear to you; only to those who have shown evidence that they can be trusted. The same is true for others. They want to know you can be trusted and that you will not let them down.

Always be truthful. Always be trustworthy. Life is better and much easier for those who live the truth. Remember the words of our friend Mark Twain, "If you always tell the truth you never have to remember anything."

DEPENDING ON YOU

Several years ago, when I was on the pastoral staff of a church, one of my responsibilities was to oversee several ministries in the church. One of these ministries was working with the ushers and welcoming crew. There was a young man who was very excited to help. Jason (not his real name) was a very pleasant young fellow. He was polite, outgoing and very eager to help in any way he could. At first, I thought he was a gift from God to help in this area of ministry. Anyone who has ever worked with a volunteer staff knows it is hard to get and keep hard working people.

It did not take long before I made a hard discovery. Jason, despite his enthusiasm and personal skills, could not be depended on. He would volunteer to help in a service or greeting as people entered the church, but did not show up at the appointed time, and many times not at all. Jason always was apologetic and had excuses for his absents, however, that did little good for those who had to fill the hole he left.

It was soon apparent we could not ask Jason to do anything that required dependability. Soon, his tasks were only to add help if he showed up. Later I found out Jason had lost several jobs for this same reason. When asked if he did not see the problem here, Jason responded with what he felt were good excuses. He had a hard time getting up, there was too much traffic, and someone in his family was sick or in need, and on and on they went. I shared with Jason a quote from Benjamin Franklin that I hoped would help him see his problem. Franklin said, "He who is good at excuses is good at little else."

Jason's difficulty with showing up is not unique to him. I have been around for quite a while now and I will say that punctuality is one of the most common struggles most people have. It is so common; we have invented tricks to help us be on time. One of the tricks I never could understand is setting the clock a head by 15 or 30 minutes so you will be on time. If you set it a head you

> "The Scoutmaster who is a hero to his boys holds a powerful lever to their development but at the same time brings a great responsibility on himself. They are quick enough to see the smallest characteristic about him, whether it be a virtue or a vice."
>
> **Sir Robert Baden-Powell**
> **1857-1941**
> **Founder of The Boy Scouts**

know it is not the real time. I have seen many who do this end up later than they would normally be because they know they have extra time so they dilly-dally it away. Why not accept that you must be on time and schedule your self-according?

Another trick is when you have a friend or family member that is always late, you tell them they must be there a half-an-hour before they really have to be. Again, they know this so they feel they have the extra time and still end up late. Here is the truth. You cannot change time one way or another. The problem many people have is not the clock it is their manners.

In Scouting, it is stressed that being on time is part of being trustworthy. People trust those who they know they can depend on. If you have a schedule to keep and many people depending on that schedule, it only takes one person to mess it all up. No one wants to be that person.

It is hard for some to see that punctuality is, in fact, nothing less than good manners. Your lateness is not hurting you, but those who depend on you to be on time. A lack of punctuality delays everything that is being done. It steals the time from others, keeps them from doing their best, and it often can hurt or destroy a project that means something to the others involved. English clergyman, Richard Cecil (1748-1810) said, "If I have made an appointment with you, I owe you punctuality, I have no right to throw away your time if I do my own."

The problem of not being on time does not just affect you. It can cause others, who do keep their promises to be on time, to be late as well. A lack of punctually shows that you have a disregard for the time of others, their business and their friendship. Punctuality is, as an author, Thomas Chandler Haliburton called it, "the soul of business." More jobs have been lost to a lack of punctuality than to a bad economy.

I got my first job at the age of 14. I washed dishes at a restaurant not far from my home for $0.50 an hour (in 1964 that was not a bad wage for a kid). My boss, Tony, gave me some advice that I remember to this day. He would tell all the staff, "If you are on time, you're late." What he expected was for us to be ready to work at our appointed time, not just arriving to work. My shift started at 4:00 pm. Tony always looked for me at 3:55 pm, and I was there. During the 4 years I had that job, I went from washing dishes to a manager position. . I also went from 50 cents to 5 dollars an hour (again, in 1968 that was good money for a kid).

Never take time, yours or anyone else's, for granted. Keep in mind that time is the one thing that cannot be replaced. Once it is gone it can never be returned. You cannot find or create extra time. You cannot save time. You cannot store up time. You have 60 seconds in a minute, 60 minutes in an hour, 24 hours in a day. Everyone who has ever lived or ever will live has the very same amount. Time is the one truly level ground for all humanity.

It is an inexcusable and moral failing to waste your time. It is a crime to waste the time of others. It is like stealing from their life. If someone has to wait an extra hour for you to show up, you cannot, no matter how much you try, replace that hour for him or her. It is gone.

A Scout learns to be trustworthy is more than telling the truth or not stealing. A Scout is dependable and one who keeps his word. If you say you will meet someone at a certain time, it is your responsibility to be sure you are there. Do whatever planning you must to make that happen, but make it happen. We are going to be talking about being prepared; part of being prepared is to know what you need to do to be on time before you must be there.

So what to do when someone keeps you waiting? When I had people coming to me for coaching I would often have to deal with those who were late or did not show at all. I am a person who is usually early for any appointment (thanks to Tony). The down side to this is that when others are late you notice it more. I also like to use my time wisely and sitting around waiting is not the best use of my time. Rather than get upset with this I have taken responsibility for my own life and created a few, time-saving and stress relieving habits that help.

If someone is coming to my office for an appointment, I do not stop working till they arrive. If they are 10 or 15 minutes late, I was able to get 10 or 15 minutes more of work done. It is my policy that if they are 30 minutes late they are rescheduled for a time they can make it. This way I have not lost that time and I keep working. There are those times when the unexpected happen. When I get a call that the person may be late or are unable to make it, I will work with them to make the needed changes. Either way, I have been working and not sitting around waiting.

If an appointment is outside the office, meeting for lunch or at a different location, I always bring a book along with pen and paper. This way, if I must wait I can use my time productively. Soon as the person arrives I am ready to go and no time has been wasted, at least not my time.

No one likes to wait. However, you must remember you have full power and responsibility for your life. Do not surrender that power of your time to other people. Simple planning and the use of common sense can help you always be in control. Your time is your own to control. That way you do not get stressed, angry or resentful toward others.

KEEPING TIME

Be prepared! That is the Boy Scout motto and should be the motto of all success-minded people. Why? Because only the prepared can be ready to make the most of each day as they travel on their journey to achievement. If you are not prepared for what may happen during your day - good or bad - you will not be able to make the most of it.

Preparing for your tomorrow is always based on how you handle your today. You must do well today if you hope to have a successful tomorrow. Too many people think they can put things off, relax and let down their guard or only give a little today and make up for it tomorrow, but that is not

"Be Prepared... the meaning of the motto is that a scout must prepare himself by previous thinking out and practicing how to act on any accident or emergency so that he is never taken by surprise."

Sir Robert Baden-Powell
1857-1941
Founder of The Boy Scouts

how it works. The great coach, John Wooden (1910-2010) used to tell his players they could only give 100%. If you only gave 80% today, you could not give 120% tomorrow. The best anyone can do is 100% and if you do not give that you lose the rest.

One of the challenges we often face in Scouting is that of sports. I say challenge because there are times when practice and games cut into what would be a Scouting activity. Scouts are encouraged to be a part of sports in school. The principles of teamwork, fair play and sportsmanship are all used in their activities. Scouts commit to doing their best, not just with things pertaining to Scouting, but their best in all things.

Sports are great for young people to learn how to handle their time and how to strive for excellence. Just as they find with any Scouting advancement or activity, they must practice and give 100% all the time if they are to win. I believe this is why so many Scouts and former Scouts have achieved success in life. This is a principle applying to all areas of life. To be the best tomorrow you must give your best today.

Let's look at today and what you can do to make it count and be at your best tomorrow.

START STRONG

Set yourself up for a good day right from the start. Get a good night's sleep so you are well rested. Get up at a reasonable time and get ready for the day. Do not sit around half the day before you do anything to move forward. Get up, clean up, dress up and go for it!

Starting strong is having a plan on what you need to do today. The best time for this is the night before. Before you retire for the night, or at the end of your work day, look at your schedule for the following day. Write down the tasks you have to do and the degree of importance they have. This way you can start with the most important things first and work through the list. Knowing what needs to be done can save time and energy.

Start the day with a positive attitude and a can-do mindset. See the day as a gift and you can make it a great one. It is always up to you. In the words of coach John Wooden, "Be true to yourself. Make each day a masterpiece. Help others. Drink deeply from good books. Make friendship a fine art. Build a shelter against a rainy day."

END STRONG

Starting strong means ending strong. You can look back over your day and know you achieved all you needed to for that one day. There is nothing undone for tomorrow. This does not mean you have nothing to do tomorrow; each day has its own stuff. You can see you made today count.

As you end the day, take the time to plan for your tomorrow. Make your list of tasks that need to be done and their order of importance. Now you know that when tomorrow becomes today, you are prepared and will greet it with enthusiasm and energy. Get to bed at a reasonable time and get the rest you need to face the exciting adventure, which will be ahead.

Scouts, as well as all success-minded people, discover there is nothing better than to reach the end of the day and know you did your best. You can sleep a restful sleep knowing that because you did your best today tomorrow will be a great day. No matter what tomorrow may bring, you will be prepared because you did your preparing today.

CHAPTER 4

BEING FAITHFUL

(A Scout is Loyal)

"A boy can learn a lot from a dog: obedience, loyalty, and the importance of turning around three times before lying down."

Robert Benchley

1889-1945

Humorist

"A Scout is Loyal. A Scout is loyal to those whom loyalty is due."

The Boy Scout Handbook

13th Edition

Any conversation about loyalty must start with clearly defining what loyalty is and the difference between being loyal and having respect. "Loyalty is devotion and faithfulness to a cause, country, group, or person." This is how loyalty is defined in Wikipedia. Where I do agree with this definition of loyalty, I do not believe it goes far enough. One of the misconceptions of the word in today's society is that loyalty is blind. Somehow we got the idea that a person is, or should be, loyal to a cause, country, group, or person no matter what. To be truly loyal would mean you stay with this thing whether it is good or bad, right or wrong, ethical or unethical. That is not only untrue it is unreasonable.

Respect, on the other hand, can and should be given to a cause, country, group or person even if you disagree with them. Respect is the ability to recognize the position a person has and what it means. We can respect a position of authority and yet, not be loyal to the person who holds that position. You can respect a cause you disagree with by recognizing that we all have differences of opinion, but that does not mean you are loyal to that cause or even are willing to defend it.

"One aim of the Boy Scouts scheme is to revive amongst us, if possible, some of the rules of the knights of old."

Sir Robert Baden-Powell
1857-1941
Founder of The Boy Scouts

Loyalty comes from three main areas, beliefs, values, and purposes. When these three come together, a person can show great loyalty. Loyalty can be as simple as standing with a friend or doing your best for your job. It can also be as profound as giving your life for your country or suffering injustice before you would betray the trust others have in you.

The Scout Law states that a Scout is loyal to whom loyalty is due. So who is that exactly? This loyalty is given to many different people and organizations. This loyalty may look different for the young person than to the adult, however, the meaning of loyalty is the same for both. .

In the Scout Handbook, loyalty is defined like this. "Loyalty can be shown everywhere: at home, in your Troop and patrol, among your classmates at school. You can also express loyalty to the United States when you respect the flag and the government." This is solid advice for every Scout and for all success-minded people.

Loyalty should be strongest in the home, however, we all know that's not always the case. Loyalty at home begins with respect. American novelist, Richard Bach said, "The bond that links your true family is not one of blood, but of respect and joy in each other's life." Family is people who you share those qualities of loyalty: belief, values, and purpose.

I know that in a perfect world, our family would be the people we are closest to in all the universe. In many cases that's true. We love our family and live in a state of gratitude that God, in His wisdom, gave them to us. However, the family is also the place where some have experienced their greatest hurts in life. People have suffered abuse at the hands of family members. Families have been broken, divided and been the home of great pain and destruction.

Yet, through all this, I have also seen great loyalty in families – even broken ones. That connection of love and caring can be greater than any bond known to human kind. That kind of loyalty is never wrong or misplaced, it's what family is all about.

We all have our groups of friends and associates that play an important part in our lives. To the Scout it is their Troop and patrols, to the success-minded person, it is their group of friends and co-workers. This can be our church or a social group we belong to, whatever the case, that loyalty of friendship is great and solid.

Young people understand the loyalty that exists among friends. Their friends play such an important role in their lives. They help define who the young person is and a feeling of belonging. The same is true for adults. The groups we belong to, whether at work, church, or social groups and organization,, help us feel that we belong and we are a part of something bigger than ourselves. The sense of loyalty we have for these groups along with the knowledge that they are loyal to us as well, give us a feeling of secutiry and fulfillment as a person.

The loyalty we have for our country is a bit deeper. Do not get this confused with loyalty to the government. There is an old quote (not sure anyone knows where it really came from), that says, "I love my country, but I fear my government." This is not our form of government, but the people who have taken, or were given, control of it.

It is the difference between loyalty to our country and that of government that gives us the freedom of election. If you disagree with someone in government, you can vote for those you would want to see there instead. Americans are loyal to the system of government that allows us to choose those who rule over us. We are loyal to the freedoms and rights we have as citizens of this great nation and we are willing to fight and give our all to protect it. This is called patriotism, and there is no greater loyalty known to human kind.

So what is it that binds us to something or someone in loyalty? There is a glue that holds it all together. Again, that glue is made up of beliefs, values, and purpose.

LOYALTY COMES FROM SHARED BELIEFS

Everything we do and fight for is based on the things we believe to be true. We are loyal to those who share our beliefs because we know they are fighting for the same causes we find important. When we are asked to stand, fight for and defend things that we do not believe in, we become weak and ineffective. Likewise, when we are following a leader who stands for the things we believe in, we become strong, committed and loyal to the end.

LOYALTY COMES FROM SHARED VALUES

The success-minded person will not be loyal to someone who is not honest, of poor character or untrustworthy. These are some of the values that make the success-minded person who they are. Many have been asked to do things that are dishonest, bend the rules or tell a white lie, but have left their job or position because to betray their values is a crime greater than any they can accept.

LOYALTY COMES FROM SHARED PURPOSES

It is hard if not impossible to be loyal to someone or something that does not share your purpose. If you want to see a person of character stand strong, give them a purpose they can believe in and stand up for. Take it away and you will have no commitment at all. The purpose is one thing that gives us drive and motivation to do what is necessary to succeed at anything in life.

REAL LOYALTY

When we are loyal, it means we have recognized our duty to something or someone. Duty is a force that keeps us on track in spite of the difficulties we face or the effort it takes. Once a Scout

> "The spirit is there in every boy; it has to be discovered and brought to light."
> **Sir Robert Baden-Powell**
> **1857-1941**
> **Founder of The Boy Scouts**

or a success-minded person understands and accepts their duty, it is only a matter of doing it, never a question of if they will do it.

As a Scout, our duty is often simple and non-threatening. As an adult, our duty becomes very real, difficult and sometimes dangerous. It is our duty all the same and, although it may be simple, it has great meaning and purpose. Former British Prime Minister, Sir Winston Churchill (1874-1965) put it well when he said, "All great things are simple, and many can be expressed in a single word: freedom, justice, honor, duty, mercy, and hope."

In our life, we have four main areas of duty that we must never forget. On these will hang our life, liberty, and success. To lack loyalty in any of these areas is to show ourselves as disloyal people.

1) OUR DUTY TO GOD

Our culture tends to think of God as religion. That means our duty would be to go to church and maybe pray when we are in need. Religion has nothing to do with duty. Every person on the planet are here because God chose to place them here. What you choose to believe is irrelevant to the fact that God is God and He is calling the shots. To do our duty to Him is to obey His word and live for Him. We serve a God of love, power, and great mercy, but we serve Him, He does not serve us. Jesus came to bring us forgiveness for sin so that we could, in fact, have a relationship with God. He also came as an example of what that relationship should look like.

As a Scout, young people are taught that their duty to God goes deeper than just attending church. They, even though they are young, have a responsibility to perform in their religious life. It is the duty of the Scout to see that those responsibilities are fulfilled with care and excellence. Our duty to God is on going throughout life. It is never completed and it is never to be neglected.

2) OUR DUTY TO OUR FAMILY

One of the tragedies of today's culture is the breakdown of the family. There is no greater joy and fulfillment than a solid family. Our duty is to be the best we can be for our family. We serve our family and care for them above our own needs. Each member of the family doing this brings love, harmony and a peace that is beyond all we could hope for. I know this sounds a bit pie-in-the-sky, but you will see that fulfilling your duty to the family will not be a chore, but a joy.

Scouts, as well as success-minded people, understand that each member of the family has a role to play. This role is vital to the success and well being of the family as a whole. Scouts are taught never to shirk their responsibility to their family by doing chores, helping when needed and following the guidance and instruction of parents. For adults, this means they take their role as a parent, protector, and provider to the family seriously and care for their children, as well as each other before their own needs.

3) OUR DUTY TO OUR EMPLOYER

This may seem out of place, however, one of the breakdowns in our society has been the lack of work ethic. Workers have begun to believe they are in control and they set the amount of work they will do and what they get paid. If you have a job, you were given that job, you get paid, and you must work. Our duty is to be a good hard worker and give more than expected of us. Yes, employers need to be fair and honest and pay their workers what they deserve.

Work ethic is not about how much you get for the job you do, it is about the job you do. Hard work is really one of the most important keys to happiness and success in life. Scouts are taught that hard work will lead them to their dreams in life. Without the work, there is no dream. As the great Brazilian soccer player, Pele said, "Success is no accident. It is hard work, perseverance, learning, studying, sacrifice and most of all, love of what you are doing or learning to do."

4) OUR DUTY TO OUR COUNTRY

We live in the greatest land in all of history. America is the place of freedom, individual exceptionalism and the ability to become whatever you wish. I know that in recent years we have gone through some hard times, however, America is still there and those who believe in her will do their duty to protect, build and keep her free.

Scouts learn that their greatest duty to our nation is not how we vote, paying taxes or even going off to war. It is to be a good citizen; that will cover all the bases and will make the country better as a whole. A great country is not a mass of people; it is made up of individual citizens doing what is right and working together to improve the country as a whole. As American anthropologist, Margaret Mead (1901-1978) said, "Never believe that a few caring people can't change the world. For, indeed, that's all who ever have."

MORE THAN A JOB

There was a time when a person found a job and worked at it for the rest of their working life. That time is long past. Today, a person may have four, five or even more careers during their time of work. Personally, I think this is the better way. We are – or should be – constantly growing, learning and making new discoveries in our lives. The thing that has not – or should not – change is the value of work itself. You need a job for far more than just making a living.

> "If you make yourself indispensable to your employer, he is not going to part with you in a hurry no matter what it costs him."
> **Sir Robert Baden-Powell**
> **1857-1941**
> **Founder of The Boy Scouts**

Now the question must be asked, why, in a piece about loyalty are we talking about work? It is because few things help us develop the character qualities that show loyalty better than the workplace. We have talked a bit about this already, however, the lessons we can learn are many, but even more are the life habits that are formed by both working and not working.

Work gives us a sense of responsibility and the ability to better the lives of our family, community and ourselves. Work is important to our health and well-being and the health and well-being of our community as well. Therefore, you will find more unhealthy people, with destructive habits and lack of motivation for improvement among those who live an idle life.

"Being busy does not always mean real work." Inventor Thomas Edison (1847-1931) said. "The object of all work is production or accomplishment and to either of these ends, there must be forethought, system, planning, intelligence, and honest purpose, as well as perspiration. Seeming to do is not doing." We have all known people, or maybe we have been guilty ourselves, who seem to be always on the go but never really accomplishing anything. These are the people who will tell you of all they plan to do and yet never really do anything.

Scouts learn that wanting to earn rank or merit badges is never enough to get you there. If you want the reward, you have to do the work. This principle is carried on to their work life. Scouts find that work is something you do, do often and do to the best of their ability.

Why does work get such a bad rap? People complain about work, avoid work and do as little work as possible. Work is not a punishment nor is it the result of the fallen state of mankind. Some people work very hard at doing as little work as possible. Some work most of their lives for the possibility of not having to work again. It is all a great mystery as to why we see common work as the enemy to ease and prosperity, when it is work that brings them into being.

Some people will do their best to avoid work simply because they are lazy. They will spend hours doing nothing at all in hopes that someone will take care of them. Sadly, that is what happens all too often. It is the old story that those who work, end up caring for those who do not. Every day, hard-working Americans see their money was taken away from them - money they have earned - and have it given to lazy Americans who could work, but do not.

So why is it that some see work as a curse that should be avoided at all costs and some see it as a gift that blesses and completes their life? It is not hard to see that it comes down to one important quality, attitude. Those with a positive attitude see work as something to embrace and go after. Those with a negative attitude see work as punishment and unnecessary. Think about it, how many lazy people do you know that are upbeat and positive, not many at all.

I want to look at a few reasons why some welcome work and do all they can to make it part of their life. Those who avoid work are not hard to figure out and therefore we do not have to use our time to exam them. It is the person who desires work that we want to not only understand, but emulate.

WORKERS SEE THAT WORK BRINGS MORE THAN MONEY

One reason some people do not like to work is that they see work is nothing more than a paycheck. Since it is far too easy to get money without the work, they opt to sit around and get paid for nothing. Workers, on the other hand, see work as far more than a pay check. Yes, work has a financial reward and for those who work hard to earn it. That financial reward can be enough to get by or a great abundance depending on the work done.owever, workers gain much more from their daily tasks. They gain a feeling of self-respect, confidence, and self-sufficiency. They know they can take care of themselves and what they have they earned. Nothing is given to them, but rather they have the great satisfaction of knowing what they have is truly theirs.

One of the principles we will talk about in the ninth point of the Scout Law, A Scout is Thrifty, is the importance of being able to pay your own way. For the Scout, earning money has a purpose. The same should be true for the success-minded person. You earn money not just to have it or the things you buy with it, you earn it to pay your own way in life.

WORKERS RESPECT THEMSELVES AND OTHERS

Workers have the joy of self-respect. I say joy because there is a great feeling that comes with knowing you have contributed to the betterment of yourself and those around you. Workers also tend to respect others and their efforts. They take care of the things they have and will respect and care for the property of others as well. When you earn your own way, you understand the value of things and what it took to gain them. It is not hard to see the difference in how those who work care for themselves and what they own, compared to those who do not.

I believe one of the reasons those who earn the Scout rank of Eagle often go on to do great things, is that to get that rank, they must earn it themselves. They get encouragement from leaders and help from fellow Scouts, but the real work, the job itself, is one they decide on, put in order and do the work. They know the joy of earning something and that joy never leaves you.

WORKERS FIND FULFILLMENT IN LIFE

Most workers are working to achieve a dream they have. That dream is different for each person, but what he or she has in common is the fact they work for a purpose. There is little in life that is more fulfilling than the achievement of one's dreams and goals. It is a great satisfaction to know that you can do anything if you are willing to work for it. And hard workers are willing to work for their dreams.

American statesman and Scout, Colin Powell said, "A dream doesn't become reality through magic; it takes sweat, determination, and hard work." He learned this lesson while a Scout and it carried him to an honorable career being a 4 star General in the U.S. Army, all the way to Secretary of State. General Powell is an excellent example that if you are willing to work hard, all things are possible.

> "When you want a thing done, 'Don't do it yourself' is a good motto for Scoutmasters."
>
> **Sir Robert Baden-Powell**
> **1857-1941**
> **Founder of The Boy Scouts**

WORKERS SEEK A BETTER LIFE

Those who work do so because they seek something better than what they have. They may want a new home or other important possessions.

Some want to get their children a good education or to have enough money to do what they have always dreamed of doing. Whatever it is, it is always moving them forward and never backwards. Each day offers them the opportunity to be better, to achieve more and realize their dreams. They have learned the principle put forth by American writer, Elbert Hubbard (1859-1915), "The best preparation for good work tomorrow is to do good work today."

Allow me to make something clear; I know there are those in our society who cannot work for many reasons. Some need the help of others to survive and that is understandable. You will find the greatest givers are those who have earned what they must give. In this great and prosperous country of ours, no one who is honestly in need should go without the basic needs of a good life. All people should have food, shelter, protection and basic needs fulfilled. However, the majority of individuals in this country on welfare are fully capable of working and simply choose not to. This may seem hard to come down on them like this, but I believe it is more cruel and distasteful to allow people who could be productive and self-sufficient to become dependent on others to live.

Work is a gift and a blessing. There is so much more here at stake than just money. We will be a stronger, more moral and far better country, when we have most people working, rather than most of them dependent on a government that sees them as sheep, rather than people. I believe as well, that the majority of people want to work. They desire to be on their own, to decide their own future and to pay their own way.

MISTAKES MAYBE, BETRAYALS NEVER

No matter if you are a Scout or Scouter, male or female, rich or poor, educated or uneducated, there is nothing more dreaded in this world than being betrayed. We can deal with most difficulties in life, even tragedies, but to be betrayed is beyond the limits for most of us. We all could repeat the words of civil rights activist, Malcolm X: "To me, the thing that is worse than death is a betrayal. You see, I could conceive death, but I could not conceive betrayal."

I believe the reason betrayal is so difficult is before you can be betrayed you must love, trust, and believe in the person or group who has betrayed you. We may not like being hurt or schemed against by those we have no relationship with and no trust in, but we can handle it. However, when that hurt or scheming comes from those we love and trust the wound is often too deep to heal.

As with most harsh lessons in life, we, as success-minded people, have something to learn here. It is painful and difficult to be betrayed. It is close to unforgivable to be the betrayer. Loyalty is the recognition that to betray others is far worse than being betrayed yourself. After all, as a writer, Isaac Bashevis Singer (1902-1991) stated, "When you betray somebody else, you also betray yourself."

We all make mistakes; that is not an excuse, but a truth. There may be a time when we say something we should not or when someone we care about does the same. This is not a betrayal it is a mistake. A betrayal is deliberated and purposeful, but mistakes are a lack of judgment, a slip of the tongue or just a plain stupid move. All of which, although hurtful and unpleasant, can and should be forgiven.

I would like for us to look at three areas where both mistakes happen most. When we are aware of the dangers, we can avoid them. That is true for both issues. If you know how to handle yourself in each situation, you can be sure not to make those painful mistakes, that is all part of being prepared. Also, if you know the places where betrayal lives, you can be ready to avoid them and the betrayers who live there.

KEEPING A SECRET

We all have secrets that we do not want to be revealed to the world. It may be a mistake we made that can cause hurt or shame to ourselves or to those we love if brought out into the open. It may be a project we are working on and we need the secrecy to keep it from running into delays or interference. It may also be a problem or difficult situation that someone else is having and it was told to us in confidence. Whatever the reason, the bottom line is the same, we do not want the world to know.

Scouts see this ability to keep and protect secrets as both being trustworthy and loyal. Trust is the key to all great relationships. Author, Stephen Covey (1932-2012) said, "Trust is the glue of life. It's an essential ingredient in effective communication. It's the foundational principle that holds all relationships."

Many good friendships or family connection has been destroyed due to the inability of one person not being able to keep a secret. I mean, how difficult is it to just keep something to yourself? The fact is there are many people who tell secrets like it's an addiction they cannot control. When told a secret they cannot wait to tell someone else what they know.

This telling of secrets is done in several ways. Some will act like the person they are telling is a "close friend" and the first thing they say is, "I trust you not to tell anyone." Others pretend it "slipped out" as if it was only a mistake, when the whole time they could not wait to tell others. And, the one I have seen repeatedly. As Christians, how many times have you heard that the secret was something they needed prayer about? Do we really think that God doesn't already know?

Success-minded people, as well as Scouts, need to use some basic common sense when it comes to keeping secrets and telling secrets. First off, if you have a friend or family member who tells you a secret they have heard, you should know never to tell that person anything you want kept secret. If they will tell you other's secrets they will tell your secrets to others.

"Juvenile crime is not naturally born in the boy, but is largely due either to the spirit of adventure that is in him, to his own stupidity, or to his lack of discipline, according to the nature of the individual."

Sir Robert Baden-Powell
1857-1941
Founder of The Boy Scouts

Be very selective on what you tell people. Ask yourself, "Do I really have to tell anyone about this at all?" I understand that there are times when we just want to talk to someone, but make that someone a person you know you can trust. And make that secret your own and not someone else's.

Secondly, if someone tells you something in confidence, do not even think about sharing it with others. We all need people we can trust and depend on, be that person. If this secret you hear is something that is illegal, or you know the person or someone else could face harm, then you have a responsibility to tell the person you cannot keep this to yourself. Actually, it may be best to do this before you hear what they are keeping secret.

Here is the bottom line, be a person who can be trusted to keep a secret. This should be in business, friendships, family matters or any other area of life. Never fall into the trap of thinking that people will be impressed that you know something they do not. If you are effectively keeping a secret, no one will even know that you know anything at all.

Breaking a confidence bond is too many a great betrayal. It is most likely one of the top reasons people feel betrayed. If for some reason you make a mistake and share something you should not, go to the person whose secret it is and tell them and apologize. As I said, we all make mistakes and we must face up to them and do what we can to make it right.

DEFEND AND PROTECT

Several years ago, a friend came to me and told me some of my co-workers were talking about me in the break room. What they were saying was hurtful and even worse, untrue. "I thought you should know." I know that my friend was thinking they did me some big favor. However, more than the hurt I felt from those who talked about me, was the hurt from my friend who felt telling me this bit of information was okay.. I also questioned in my head, "Why did you not defend me?"

A loyal friend is more than someone who will not talk about you. They are a person who, when they hear you being defamed, will come to your defense. A lesson we try to stress in Scouting is that you do not talk about your friends or anyone behind their back. Also, when you hear this kind of talk, make it clear you do not want to be a part of it and be willing to stand up for your friends when they are not there to defend themselves.

Gossip has no place in the life of a Scout or the success-minded person. Gossip does nothing but hurt and destroy. You gain no knowledge or helpful information from gossip. American clergyman, Lawrence Lovasik (1913-1986) put it well when he said, "It is just as cowardly to judge an absent person as it is wicked to strike a defenseless one. Only the ignorant and narrow-minded gossip, for they speak of persons instead of things."

Once you have gotten a reputation, (and you will get one) as a person who does not tolerate gossip and is there to defend his friends, people will go out of their way not to gossip when you are around. That is good for you, good for them and it cleans a bit more dirt out of the world.

KEEP YOUR WORD

We did talk about this a little bit in our discussion on being trustworthy, but I feel it is important enough to touch on here as well. Being a person of your word is far more than showing up at the time you said you would. It goes beyond performing a task you said you would do. It is living the life you have said you would live. Being the person you have promised you would be.

There is something to be said for taking an oath. It drives home the reality of what you are promising to do. This is one reason why I love the Scout Oath and Law, the Scout Oath starts with the words, "On my honor..." This means that the Scout is promising, even more than promising, their honor is on the line here. This is serious business.

The great American General, Douglas Mac Arthur said, "Duty, Honor, Country. Those three hallowed words reverently dictate what you ought to be, what you can be, what you will be."

Scouts understand it is not the goal to memorize, "On my honor, I will do my best to do my duty to God and my country and to obey the Scout Law; to help other people at all times; to keep myself physically strong, mentally awake, and morally straight." The goal is to live that promise every day of their lives. I have said many times now, but I want to stress the importance so I will say it again. Boy Scouts is not just for when a boy is young and wants something to do. It is a life course that will be with them as long as they live. The desire is to instill these principles in young boys so they will grow to be the best of men.

The Mission of the Boy Scouts is clear, "The mission of the Boy Scouts of America is to prepare young people to make ethical and moral choices over their lifetimes by instilling in them the values of the Scout Oath and Law."

As you can see, keeping their word is essential to being a Scout. Likewise, keeping your word as to how you will live your life is essential to being a success-minded person. Every person who desires to be their best and make the world a better place, should also understand and take this oath. You do not need to be a Scout to follow the Scout Oath and Law, you only need to be a person of honor and duty.

GOD, FAMILY, AND COUNTRY

Some of you older readers may remember a day when it was encouraged to be a good citizen. I can even remember when you got a good citizenship award in school. Now you are fortunate to find a person who can even tell you what a good citizen is.

The Merriam-Webster Dictionary defines it as the qualities that a person is expected to have as a responsible member of a community. These "qualities" are like those of good manners, you know them when you see them, but you don't see them a lot. Too often people are too busy looking out for their right, their entitlements, and their stuff to worry about the rights of others. But like good manners, citizenship is all about others first, not me first.

One of the personal lessons I was not really prepared for as a Cub Scout leader was finding out most boys did not understand what citizenship was. The idea of protecting the rights of others, following the Constitution and the order of law were concepts they were not taught in school or at home. Yet, without good citizens, we have no country.

Being a good and productive citizen is something each of us must strive to achieve. There are many ways we can accomplish this. One is to follow the laws and do what is right, not because there is a penalty if you do not, but because it is the right thing to do.

Another important part of being a good citizen, that far too many have allowed to fall aside, is to be involved in government. I am not talking about complaining about government or posting your political views on social media. To be involved means we are taking an active part in our local, state and national government. Run for office, volunteer or work in a position that will cause change and promote good, citizens.

> "One of the finest statesmen of the present time is also a first-class scout, and that is Mr. Roosevelt, the late President of the United States of America."
>
> **Sir Robert Baden-Powell**
> **1857-1941**
> **Founder of The Boy Scouts**

We could go on forever talking about the wrong there is in our government today (and there is a lot wrong). How they are dishonest, lack integrity and that our rights as citizens are being taken from us. But all that talk, no matter how right it is, means nothing if we do not make the changes needed. We still have a government chosen by the people. So, how do we make it better? We become the people who hold the offices.

The days when we believed anyone could become President are not over. It can happen if we insist that it happens. Good citizens do not sit back and give up they fight for the right. Good citizens do not wait for change they make the change. We can change our city, state, and country for the better. By doing so, we teach those youngsters coming up that they too can make a difference. Remember, the future belongs to them, let's make it better now so they can make it great once more.

CHAPTER 5

BEING USEFUL

(A Scout is Helpful)

"You can read clever motivational sayings all day, but that won't replace you getting off your butt and doing the hard work."

Darren Hardy
Author/Publisher

"A Scout is helpful. A Scout cares about other people. He helps others without expecting payment or reward. He fulfills his duties to his family by helping at home."

The Boy Scout Handbook
13th Edition

Do you remember the "Help Wanted" signs? I know there are still some around, but now many are more specific like Waitress Wanted, Mechanic Wanted, Experiences (whatever) Wanted. The fact remains, businesses are looking for people to help. There is a myth that a job is hard to find, but that is not really the case. There are lots of jobs out there for people who want to help.

The third point of the Scout Law is: A Scout is Helpful. Scouts are taught to be on the lookout for things they can help others with. We are not talking about looking for a job, but for the opportunity to fore help – at no charge – to anyone who may need it. This is what is known as, A Good Deed.

In Scouting, they have a slogan, which instructs them to do a good turn daily. That means that every day they should be looking for opportunities to do something good and helpful for someone. This deed is done freely, happily, and it is done well.

"The boy is not governed by don't, but is led by do."
Sir Robert Baden-Powell
1857-1941
Founder of The Boy Scouts

It is easy for the pursuit of success to become a very self-centered journey. One of the key elements to achievement is to have a burning passion for your goal. It is what you think about, work for and plan your life around. Because of the strong attention, we give to achieving; we can forget there is another key, without which we cannot arrive at real and lasting success.

It is a paradox of life, but very true that the more you give the more you get. It is in helping others to succeed that we can truly succeed in our own life. Selfishness and self-centeredness will not lead to a successful life no matter how hard you try.

This truth is stressed in the Boy Scouts through their slogan, Do A Good Turn Daily. The Scout Handbook defines it this way, "That means doing something to help others each day without expecting anything in return." That ending is key, " without expecting anything in return." Success-minded people are to help others, do good deeds, and not expect to gain from it. As coach, John Wooden used to say, "You can't live a perfect day without doing something for someone who can never repay you."

Success-minded people should follow the Scout's example and keep their eyes open to opportunities around them each day, to do something for those they meet. This can be as simple as opening a door for someone or giving an encouraging word to a person who is struggling or it can be as involved as being a mentor to a young person or helping on a project. The size and scope of the deed are not the issues; it is the intent and attitude that makes the difference.

The act of doing good deeds will soon become a good habit in your life. You will find you do kind things for people without really thinking about it. This will transform your life for the better and bring success to a level you never thought possible. There is no getting away from it, the more you give the more you get, it is a law of nature and does not change.

Back when I was first exploring the Scout Law and how it can work in a person's life, I put the principle of doing a good deed to the test. I started looking for chances to do things, small and large, for people wherever I went. I would almost run to get to the door at the store to hold it open for the next person coming in. If someone dropped something, I was there to pick it up. If they had to reach for something, I was there to get it for them. I even carried change in my pocket to help someone who needed exact change for some reason.

Two things started happening when I did this. The first is rejection and to honest I was not expecting it, but not all people who you try to help accept it. In fact, I was called names a few times and some people just ignored me like I was not even there. I believe the idea that someone would just want to help them was not in their belief system. Sometimes when you try to help, you become suspect.

Now there were those who welcomed it, some with surprise and appreciation, but they did like being helped. It then would cause them to do something for someone else. A few years back, an insurance company had a TV commercial where a guy picked up an umbrella a lady left at a bus stop and returned it to her. She, in turn, rescues a cup of coffee a man almost spilled. This man, in turn, helps carry some packages that a person was struggling with and on and on it went. Well, that really was happening. To be honest, it was great fun to see how big a chain reaction you could cause.

The other thing these acts of kindnest impacted was myself, not to those I tried to help. I started to feel like a super hero. I was Good deed Man! Really, I loved the feeling of being helpful. I made people feel good and helped them in some way all at the same time. What started as an experiment become a way of life.

People avoid doing things for others because they think it is too much work, they will lose something or they will be taken advantage of. I have even seen this type of thinking in Scouts. I try to help them understand that, rather than being a lot of work, it is one of the most fun things I do all day. Doing a good deed can become very addictive. You start to think of creative ways to help people and challenge yourself to do more and more all the time.

As for losing something, believe me, you gain far more than you give. As I said earlier, it is a law of nature that the more you give the more you get. In

"The Scoutmaster teaches boys to play the game by doing so himself."
Sir Robert Baden-Powell
1857-1941
Founder of The Boy Scouts

it is our nature as Scouts and success-minded people to be the hero of our story. Nothing does that better than knowing you have really helped others and to know you matter.

As for being taken advantage of, that is impossible. You cannot take advantage of a person who freely gives away what you take. No one can take your helpfulness or your kindness against your will. They may be able to make you do things, but they cannot take goodness from you. You can only give it away. By giving help and kindness, you are the one in control. This truly is a super power that can change the world.

GIVING PRICELESS GIFTS

We all have heard many times that it is better to give than to receive. Depending on your age group or the degree of the self-centeredness of a person, we would agree this is true. Success-minded people find great fulfillment when they can do things for others. This can be giving help with tasks that need to be done, or giving of material resources like food or many to those in need. In Scouting, we may call this doing a good deed, but it really is the giving of special gifts. Often, when we talk of giving we tend to look at things. We give gifts, money or something we own. These are easy to give and never last for a long time. I would like to look at four gifts that keep on giving and have far greater value.

GIFT 1. YOUR TIME

Of all gifts, we can give time as the most precious. If you give a material gift, you can always replace it. If you give money, you can always get more, but when you give of your time you are giving something that cannot be replaced. Once our time is gone, whether that be a minute or a day, it is gone forever and you can never get it back. With that in mind, give your time wisely. See it as an investment in others and do not waste it. One of the great things about giving time is we all have the same amount to work with. No one has more and no one has less.

Scouts, as well as success-minded people, need to also see this gift from the viewpoint of the receiver as well as the giver. Remember when someone gives you their time they are giving you an irreplaceable gift. Respect that gift and treasure it because you cannot return it to them when you are done. It is a gift like no other, whether given or received, recognize it as the priceless gem it is.

GIFT 2. YOUR ATTENTION

When you are with someone, be with them. Do not spend the time on your phone or on a game. When people talk to you, listen to what they have to say. When you are working with them be sure to share the experience completely. I agree with the words of philosopher and writer, Henry David Thoreau (1717-1862) who said, "The greatest compliment that was ever paid me was when one asked me what I thought, and attended to my answer."

No one likes to talk to the wall. Not listening or paying proper attention to someone is not only unkind it is rude. We will address this again in the fifth point of the Scout Law A Scout is Courteous. Just keep in mind that not paying attention to someone who is talking with you is the same as receiving a gift from him or her and tossing it in the trash, while they are still there. Open the gift, you may find it very valuable to you.

GIFT 3. YOUR ENCOURAGEMENT

Life is hard. It is hard for everyone, not just you. We all need some help along the way from time to time. We need someone to believe in us and to believe we will, in fact, achieve our dreams. Be that person to those around you. If someone needs a pat on the back, a kind smile or a "You can do it!" be sure it comes from you. Believe in the greatness of others and the possibilities they hold. Always be the positive encourager, never the negative roadblock.

The road Scouts travel is paved with encouragement, they are encouraged by their leaders, as well as by their fellow Scouts. This is not because they are taught to say encouraging things, (they are actually) but because they really believe in each other. Scouts, like success-minded adults, know that each of us has great potential and as one of us succeeds, we all succeed.

GIFT 4. YOUR SKILLS

Be ready to lend a hand when people are in need. You have gifts and talents that others need. Be generous with what you have and do your best every time. You will find the more you are willing to help others, the more they will be willing to help you. We need each other, so this is a gift that gives again and again.

An important element of being helpful is not just doing things for others, but to help others to do for themselves. Scouts, like all people, have different talents and abilities. One may find a certain merit badge easy and another finds the same badge difficult. It is in helping one another that we all move forward.

YOU DON'T HAVE TO BE A TEACHER TO TEACH

Some of the greatest teachers in my life never stood before a classroom full of students; they never had a degree, nor did they study in the best universities. I have had teachers who were young (some as old as 3 years) and some old. Some have been standing by my side and some I have never met. My teachers have been well known to the world and others never heard of. And some of my teachers have been dead for ages before I was even thought of.

A teacher is someone who can teach you something and if that is the case, then every person you meet is a teacher in some way. The Scottish Philosopher, Thomas Carlyle (1795-1881) said, "Every man is my superior in that I may learn from him." Likewise, you are a teacher to every person you meet. The only question is what are you teaching?

The whole basis for Scouting is that of teaching and learning. Boys teach boys, adults teach youth, community members teach the Scouts and Scouts teach the community. At all times, you are learning and you are teaching. Skills, abilities, talents are all things to share with each other just as you freely give of your own.

So what does this have to do with being helpful? Just as we have seen in the other points of the Scout Law, the principles there are broad and cover many areas. I do not know a way to help people more than to help them learn. By helping people learn you will transform their lives forever. It is without question the most powerful tool in the Scouting toolbox.

One of the things I have loved in Scouting, as an adult, is the merit badge program. I enjoy helping young people learn some of the skills I have picked up in life and I enjoy watching them learn. I have also enjoyed learning things I never knew before. As my grandson earned his badges, I have been able to learn with him. It has been one of the best, and most useful educations I could have ever hoped for.

Here is a truth that every successful person knows, you may know a lot, but you will never know it all. You need other people to teach you what you need to be successful. People who think they are the smartest person in the room never really succeed in life. They have cut themselves off from what they need to know. If you are your best teacher, you are limited in how much you can grow. You can only know what you already know. To grow, you need to know what you do not know. Businessman, Michel Dell, who is the founder and CEO of Dell Technologies, said, "Try never to be the smartest person in the room. And if you are, I suggest you invite smarter people...or find a different room."

Teaching and learning go hand in hand, no teacher worth his/her salt is less of a student as they are a teacher. To teach you must learn and keep on learning. In fact, I would say a hardworking student could be an effective teacher. This truth applies in every area of life. Success-minded people learn all they can so they can give all they learn.

All this is well and good, but we are still faced with the age-old question, how do I make this happen? There are four main areas of learning and teaching I would like for us to look at. Each of these areas is part of our everyday life. They do not require a college education or earning a degree or certificate. Each can be done by all of us, no matter our status, income, education, beliefs or social group. In short, you can do this yourself. It is important for the success-minded person to understand that ALL useful learning and ALL useful teaching is a deliberate and purposeful act. It does not and will not happen on its own.

> "Personally, I like reading adventures which really have happened to people, because they show what kind of things might happen to oneself, and they teach one how to 'Be Prepared' to meet them."
>
> **Sir Robert Baden-Powell**
> **1857-1941**
> **Founder of The Boy Scouts**

LEARN THROUGH BOOKS / TEACH OTHERS TO READ

Throughout this book, you have heard and will continue to hear my encouragement for you to read. I believe one of the greatest gifts God has bestowed on humankind is the ability to read. Reading opens the universe to us in far deeper ways than even experience can offer. You may never climb to the top of Mt. Everest, but through reading the first-hand accounts of those who have, you can know what it was like.

Through books, we can go on great adventures, learn from the most brilliant minds in the world and understand the mysteries of the universe. If you read for just 20 minutes a day, you could read about 24 books a year. Since the average person reads about 1-2 books a year (many do not read any at all) you are way ahead of the pack. In fact, most doctrinal students do not read that many during the full course of their studies. If you read daily on the same subject, in one year you would have more knowledge on the topic than a person who spent 4 years in a classroom. Do you want to be an expert? Read, read, and read some more.

In all the information and skill, you could teach a person, nothing can be compared to the value of reading. When I say to teach a person to read, I do not necessarily mean to actually teach them to read. That may be the case from time to time, and where many in America are literate, there are still some people who cannot read.

When I talk about teaching to read, I mean to teach people the love of reading. Nothing makes me crazier than to hear an intelligent person say, "I just don't like to read." That is like saying you do not like to eat or breathe. As Mark Twain said, "The only thing sadder than a person who cannot read is a person who can and doesn't."

One thing I have found true in many young people is they think they do not like to read when in fact they do not like what they read. Once they are introduced to books on topics they enjoy or fiction they are interested in, then they discover reading is fun and helpful. There are many other deeper issues here too that I cannot get into at this time. The point is this, when you teach people to love reading, you give them the gift of freedom, adventure, and true education.

LEARN THROUGH SKILLS / TEACH OTHERS WHAT YOU KNOW

There is a big difference between talents and skills. Talents are natural, they are what can be called gifts. Some people have a natural talent for music or art or sales and dealing with people. They do this with little effort and find it easy to build on. Skill, on the other hand, is an ability you learn. You do not have to have a natural talent in an area to develop a skill.

There are times when it is hard to develop a skill without a talent to go with it. What comes to my mind first is music. For example, singing, you can learn the skills connected to singing, like how to breathe properly and use your muscles in the right way. You can learn to read music and understand the difference between a tenor and a soprano. But if you do not have the talent to sing, you will be not much more than noise. This is why a person can teach, write music and direct others to sing and yet, have little talent to do so themselves.

Skills come out strongest in the work we do. Professions like carpentry, plumbing, electrical and other skilled trades are so important. Please do not get me wrong; I am not saying these people do not have a talent. On the contrary, many are brilliant at what they do. I think what is more evident is not the talent for a trade skill, but the lack of talent. There are many people, like me, who could not drive a nail if you put it in a car. What I am saying is these skills can be taught to others.

Most every area of life is connected to a learned skill. You can learn how to be a good parent, student or teacher. You can learn communication with others, good manners, and kindness. You can learn how to perform well in any area of employment or career choice. Skills can be learned by anyone, the question is not "can I do this" but "do I want to do this?"

Put aside some time right now and take a quick inventory of your skills. What do you know how to do? What tasks do you perform at work? What are your hobbies or interests? Make a list of all the things you are skilled at. Now, think about who you can teach these skills to. How can you pass on your knowledge to others and help them in their pursuit of skill?

Another thing to remember is you never hit the end of learning a skill. You will not one day know you have learned everything there is to know on any subject. If you do feel you have learned it all, you have failed to learn much of anything. Success-minded people are ones who believe they can always get better.

> "A boy carries out suggestions more wholeheartedly when he understands their aim."
>
> **Sir Robert Baden-Powell**
> **1857-1941**
> **Founder of The Boy Scouts**

Not to be better than anyone else, but to be the best they can be personally. Yes, that may be better than anyone else, however, being better than other people is never the goal, bettering yourself is always the goal.

Over the past few years, actor, Mike Rowe, an Eagle Scout, has risen to be the main voice for the skilled trades in this country. One of the things that Rowe points out and that I feel is of vital importance, is it is not a bad or less-than great thing to work hard. Rowe said, "We must change what we think of as a good education." We, especially in America, have gotten into the idea that if you do not attend a four-year college and go on to graduate school, you do not have a good education. That is a real falsehood. Many people have completed school with Masters Degrees or even Doctorates and are still unemployed, or even worse, unemployable. All they really got from their years of school is a debt they cannot pay back.

"I think a trillion dollars of student loans and a massive skills gap are precisely what happens to a society that actively promotes one form of education is the best course for the most people." Mike Rowe said, "I think the stigmas and stereotypes that keep so many people from pursuing a truly useful skill, begin with the mistaken belief that a four-year degree is somehow superior to all other forms of learning."

Out of this kind of thinking comes the idea for apprenticeships and trade schools. There are thousands of jobs, well-paying jobs, out there just waiting for those with the skills to fill them. Yes, it means work, hard work, but that is not a bad thing. Rowe points out, "We've waged war on work. We have collectively agreed, stupidly, that work is the enemy." Work is not the enemy. The answer to many of our personal issues as well as national ones is just good old decent hard work.

In Scouting, young people are given the opportunity to try many different skills during their time as a Scout. They will learn how to speak in public and lead a group of people as well as how to weld and build things from the bottom up. All this is more than just earning a badge or award for their work. It is there to teach them that hard work is its own reward. It teaches them different career choices they may have never known of. It also teaches them the responsibility to make their own choices and pursue their own paths.

Every young person should be presented with these options before they reach college age. Too often, school counselors tell students what path to follow or parents dictate the career choice of their child. By offering young people a chance to sample many different areas of skill, you allow them to find their own fit and passions in life.

LEARN THROUGH EXPERIENCE / TEACH THROUGH STORY

Everyone Loves A Good Story, that was my tagline from back in the late 90's when I was working as a professional storyteller. Back then, I was referring to fictional stories and fairy tales, however, right now, I want to talk about your real-life story. After all, we all do love a good story.

Every day you have a new story to tell. Every day you learn something new and you travel down the path of your life. I know someone is saying, "Nothing ever happens in my life. I have no story at all." That is not true. It is not that you have nothing happening, it is that you are not paying attention, the more you pay attention the more stories you have to tell.

I have always been a big advocate of journaling and I have kept one since I was 18 years old. As of today, I have 49 journals; counting the one I work in now, there is 50 years' worth. I have used these journals to look back on my life and re-discover my own stories. I, as with most humans, have faced difficult decisions and choices that I have faced before. The journal helps me see what my choices in the past were and whether they were good or bad choices. They are books of encouragement, warning, and instruction.

Along with the help, these journals have given me; my hope is to one day pass them on to my grandchildren (I have 10). I am all too aware that one day, I will no longer be around to pass on advice or to warn them that a mistake lies ahead. This will allow me to give them my lessons long after I am gone and when it comes to making mistakes to learn from, I have done well beyond my share.

Before you think I have achieved something super-human by keeping journals that many years, let me tell you, 90% is nothing but a habit. Each day I start with some devotions followed with a time to record my thoughts and feelings, it is like showering or brushing my teeth. I just do it and think little about it and I don't do it every day. To be honest, some days I have nothing to say, or the day starts off quickly and I never get to it and that is okay. I do not stress over a day I did not journal. I always have tomorrow to extend the story.

I am not saying journaling is the only way to collect your stories, but it is one of the best. I have learned long ago not to store things in my memory. The memory is a tricky thing, for one, it leaks. It is so easy to forget something that you at one time felt was important. Our memory is also not very accurate because it remembers only bit and pieces of an event or a lesson. Even worse, it will actually change the facts on you and you will remember things that really never happened at all.

The point is you want to learn from all life offers you. No matter if you journal, take notes or record them on your phone, lessons are to be used. It is only by understanding and using the lessons you get in life that you will grow, mature and become better as a person. This is where true knowledge and wisdom come. Never buy into thinking wisdom comes with old age, it only comes from learning experiences. Experiences come with age, however, if you learn from them or not, is up to you. We all know how true the old expression is, "There is no fool like an old fool."

Success-minded people see life as a classroom. They have an assignment each day to know more than when the day started, to be more than when the day started and to have improved in some way. Success-minded people try to live by the words of Benjamin Franklin

(1706-1790) who said, "Be at war with your vices, at peace with your neighbors, and let every new year find you a better man."

This improvement is important in more ways than just your betterment. It is for the betterment of those we love and can add value to their life. When faced with a difficult challenge, the lessons you have learned can help you face it with courage and the confidence you need to succeed. It also is a life lesson to those whose lives you touch. If you can make it, they can too. They will know by following the path you left for them, they can overcome just as you did.

"There are thousands of boys being wasted daily to our country through being left to become characterless, and, therefore, useless wasters, a misery to themselves and an eyesore and a danger to the nation. They could be saved if only the right surroundings or environment were given to them at the receptive time of their lives."

Sir Robert Baden-Powell
1857-1941
Founder of The Boy Scouts

The lessons we experience in life cannot be replaced and should never be forgotten. This is the best education you will get and the one that matters most. You have two responsibilities, one is to learn from your life and the other is to pass on what you have learned. Embrace the words of American musician, Dale Turner, "Some of the best lessons we ever learn are learned from past mistakes. The error of the past is the wisdom and success of the future."

LEARN THROUGH DISCIPLINE / TEACH WHAT IS RIGHT

Let's be honest, no one likes discipline. I am not talking about being punished when you do something wrong, I mean the ability to learn good habits and keep doing what you know needs to be done. As we are going through the 12 points of the Scout Law, each takes discipline to follow. Different people find different things harder than others, but all take discipline and all take work.

The great Olympic athlete, Jesse Owens (1913-1980) said, "We all have dreams. But in order to make dreams come into reality, it takes an awful lot of determination, dedication, self-discipline, and effort." Nothing great is ever achieved without the ability to discipline ourselves and do what we need to do to succeed. Discipline is action and we know, nothing happens without action.

Discipline does not come to us naturally. By nature, we look for the easy way around things. It is easier to give into our desires, distractions, and laziness than to focus, preserve and put in the hard work. A discipline is a deliberate act and something we must learn to do. It means turning away from bad habits and things keeping us from our goals and dreams. It means doing what is good and right.

As a runner, Jesse Owens had a natural talent, he loved to run and felt his best on the track. However, he would have just been another runner in a field of runners had he not understood that he needed discipline to win. Every day he practiced. He ran no matter how he felt or what the conditions were. His competition? Himself. He was always looking to beat his own records, and he had records to beat. At the Big Ten Track Meet in Ann Arbor, Michigan in 1935, Owens set three world records and went on a fourth in less than an hour later. It was known as the greatest 45 minutes in sports history.

The following year at the 1936 Olympics in Berlin, Germany, Jesse Owens won four gold medals and was the most successful athlete at the games. This did not just happen by chance. It did not happen because he had everything going his way. Actually, being a black athlete in the 1930's was not an advantage at all. He had to win by being the best at what he did, with no short cuts, no give away. He won because he was the best, plain and simple.

Success-minded people learn, as do athletes, that if you are to win in life, you must be disciplined and willing to do the hard work it takes. There are no short cuts and nothing is for free. However, if you are disciplined and have developed the habits and behaviors to move you over the top, you can do anything.

This principle of self-discipline is what Scouts learn by following the Scout Oath and Law. These are the principles of life. Every decision they make is weighted against that Law. Every time they choose to achieve something new, they follow the Law to do it right. There is never an occasion or reason for compromise. They discipline themselves to stay within the boundaries of the Oath and Law. Scouts know discipline is not restrictive, but the way to win and be the best they can be.

Olympic great, Jesse Owens was also a supporter of Scouting. Owens, who won 4 gold medals for Track & Field at the 1936 Olympic games in Berlin, Germany spent his later years traveling to Troops around the country telling his story of achievement. Jesse Owens believed that young people could achieve anything if they worked hard and learned self-discipline. He was not a Scout himself, but supported the principles taught in Scouting. Jesse stressed the importance of doing your best and following the principles of the Scout Law.

A BETTER WORLD

You are an example, whether you are working, playing, teaching or going through daily life. Others are always watching you and people do notice, despite what we may think. At work, people will see your work habits, if you are on time; do more or less than you are asked to do. At home, they notice how you treat those who you are closest to and the respect you give to others. At play or relaxing with friends, they notice the way you behave, the language you use and the things you do for fun. There is no escaping it you are an example.

Success-minded people understand true integrity is what you do when no one is looking. Why? Because it is part of whom you are as a person. It is hard work to behave properly in front of everyone, it takes focus and energy to be cautious about what you say and do to set a good example. It is not hard at all when that person you want to portray is really who you are.

A Scout is expected, not encouraged – expected to be some one who follows the Scout Oath and Law, while they are at Scouting events and when they are alone. There is never a time when a Scout is not a Scout. This may sound restrictive, but in reality, it is very freeing. Scouts do not have to think, "Am I doing what I'm supposed to be doing right now?" They will always be doing what is expected of them. Why? Because they are Scouts and that is what a Scout does.

We have already referred to the famous quote of Mark Twain, when he said, "If you always tell the truth you don't have to remember anything." That applies to our behavior as well because if you are a person of good character, integrity and kindness, you do not have to pretend for anyone. It should always be who you are. There is no acting differently for one group than another, you live as the person you really are. Honestly, trying to keep what you do with whom straight is just too much work.

Want to live in a better world? Be a better person. Want to work with people who do their best? Give more than expected and strive for excellence. Be that person. Set the standards for those around you. Not to brag or look down on people, that is the opposite of what I am asking you to do. Be an honest and real success-minded person who others can follow and see how it is done.

Never accept the excuse, "Well, no one else is doing it. Why should I be the one to be the example?" You are an example no matter what you do, so why not be a good one. You notice when people behave badly, cheat, lie and skip out on work. Why would you think people would not notice when you do it?

In the end, success-minded people believe they are here to make things better. They know they are just one person, but they are a good one. They understand that by being one less problem to the rest of the world, they have shown the path to success. If we all strive to be the best we can be, we have made a massive change that will improve the lives of many.

CHAPTER 6

BEING COMPANIONABLE

(A Scout is Friendly)

"There suddenly appeared in my world – I saw them first, I think, in 1908 – a new sort of little boy – a most agreeable development of the slouching, cunning, cigarette-smoking, town-bred youngster; a small boy in khaki hat, and with bare knees and athletic bearing, earnestly engaged in wholesome and invigorating games up to and occasionally a little beyond his strength – the Boy Scout. I liked the Boy Scout."

H.G. Wells

1866-1946

Author

"A Scout is friendly. A Scout is friendly to all. He is a brother to other Scouts. He offers his friendship to people of all races, religions, and nations, and he respects them even if their beliefs and customs are different from his own.

The Boy Scout Handbook
13th Edition

Pastor, radio host and educator, Charles Swindoll said, "I cannot even imagine where I would be today were it not for that handful of friends who have given me a heart full of joy. Let's face it, friends make life a lot more fun." I must agree with this wholeheartedly. Without the love and support of good friends, I don't know where I would be. It has also been my

"The Good Turn will educate the boy out of the groove of selfishness."

Sir Robert Baden-Powell
1857-1941
Founder of The Boy Scouts

desire to be such a friend to others and I have been blessed with some great examples.

Scouting is all about friendship. Young people place a great importance on having friends. Their approval and acceptance make all the difference in the world to them and that's why the young are so often victims of peer pressure. This is also why it is vital they have the right friends who will "pressure" them into doing the right things. Scouts have a bond that helps them feel they belong, they are accepted and are not on their own.

Friendship is more than just the fact you know each other. We see people every day, at work, school, church or wherever, and we greet each other and are pleasant, but that does not really make us friends. Friends are those who are involved in our lives and we in theirs. A friend is a person you talk with, laugh with, cry with, and believes in. Nineteenth-century English Clergyman, Robert Hall (1764-1831), described a friend this way, "A friend should be one in whose understanding and virtue we can equally confide, and whose opinion we can value at once for its justness and its sincerity." Let's look at four ways you can be this kind of a friend.

1) FRIENDS BELIEVE IN EACH OTHER

It is one thing to agree with the dreams and ambitions of your friends and another to believe in those dreams and ambitions. As a friend, believe in the dreams of those you care about. Some may be a bit far out there and you may not fully understand, but they are not your dreams to understand. Know that your friend has this dream and your place, as their friend, is not to critique or remodel it, but rather support and believe in them.

Scouts often share their dreams with other Scouts. They find their Scouting friends are not only accepting of their hopes and dreams, but encouraging and helpful to them in achieving them. It is easy to see the best in others when you believe the best of them. If you believe your friend can do the impossible, they seldom let you down.

2) FRIENDS SHARE THEIR DREAMS

Just as you are willing to hear and believe in your friend's dream, allow them to be apart of yours. If the relationship is all one sided, then it is not a healthy relationship in the first place. One of the marks of a real friend is you will make each other better people and achievers. As a businessman, Henry Ford said, "My best friend is the one who brings out the best in me."

Encouragement is a two-way street, Scouts not only support and encourage their friends to achieve, but they get that encouragement back again. When Scouts succeed, they succeed together.

3) FRIENDS ACCEPT NOTHING LESS THAN EXCELLENCE

A true friend is one who knows you have the potential to be excellent in all you do and will accept nothing less. I have heard many times that a true friend accepts you just the way you are, but that is not at all true. The waiter in the restaurant or the bank teller accepts you "just as you are." They don't care what you do or how you live. A true friend cares about you and will do all they can to keep you from doing things that will injure your character or reputation. Friends will always work to help you become the very best you can be and not ignore your flaws, but help you overcome them.

The Scout Law is the standard for each and every Scout. I have found that the ones, who hold their friends to that standard, are Scouts more than adults. It is not a club that they hit each other with, but a guide they use to show direction and instruction. A Scout does not only live by the Scout Oath and Law, but they help their friends to do so as well.

4) FRIENDS ARE ENCOURAGERS

"When you encourage others, you in the process are encouraged because you're making a commitment and difference in that person's life." Zig Ziglar (1926-2012), author and speaker said, "Encouragement really does make a difference." There is no greater gift we can give to our friends, family or to ourselves than that of encouragement. Sometimes it is as simple as a warm smile and a soft pat on the back, other times it means sitting quietly with a hurting friend, just so they know you are there. If you have one gift to give to your friends, let it be encouragement.

Scouting is great, but you can get discouraged from time to time. There is so much you are trying to achieve and it can all get overwhelming. This is where their Scouting friends come in, they encourage each other in so many ways. Some will give words of encouragement like, "You can do it," or "I know you got this one." Others pitch in and help with a difficult task or project. Still others will check in outside of Scouting events, to help keep each other accountable. Whatever they do, they encourage their friends and in turn, are encouraged themselves.

"When a boy finds someone who takes an interest in him, he responds and follows."
Sir Robert Baden-Powell
1857-1941
Founder of The Boy Scouts

I NEED A FRIEND

Friendship is one of the undervalued treasures of life. When you have friends, you have all the elements that are needed to achieve success. There is support, guidance, encouragement, and help. Those with few friends are poor, but those with many are wealthy. Presidential candidate, and former Vice President, Hubert H. Humphrey (1911-1978) said, "The greatest gift of life is friendship, and I have received it."

Knowing this profound truth, why do so many have a difficult time developing and maintaining friendships? The most common mistake people make about friendship is thinking it is about them and how their friends treat them. Friendship is always about our friends and how good a friend we are to them.

When we say, a Scout is friendly; we are not saying a Scout looks for friendly people. Scouts, as well as success-minded people, understand that to have a friend, you first have to be a friend. You do not worry about what you can get from others, you first think about what you can give to them. A friend is a giver of value, not just a taker of time.

Let me share with you a few key elements to a good and solid friendship that you can apply to your life. These will make you a better friend and will increase your ability to gain more friends.

HAVE A POSITIVE ATTITUDE

Nothing will repel friends faster than a grumpy and moody disposition. Who wants to be around a sour puss? Those who gain friends are those who are pleasant and cheerful. People like to be around happy and positive people, they want to feel encouraged and excited about life and your attitude can make that happen.

For whatever reason, young men often walk around like they have a chip on their shoulder. They do not smile and always seem mad at the world. This often puzzled me because if there is ever a time to be positive and happy it is when you are young. This attitude problem is not excluded from Scouts. I have seen many Scouts who looked like they would bite your face off if you got too close. I have also seen their attitude change after time at a Scouting event or camping trip. Why? Because they discover that being positive is more fun than being grumpy. They discover what singer/song writer, Willie Nelson said, "Once you replace negative thoughts with positive ones, you'll start having positive results."

CARE FOR OTHERS

The selfish and self-centered do not make good friends. They spend all their time thinking about themselves and what they want and think nothing of anyone else. A good friend cares about other people more than themselves and they know how to listen, to encourage and enjoy the hopes and dreams of others. A good friend does all they can to help their friends achieve and grow.

Our young people are growing up in one of the most self-centered times in history. They are told on every side to lookout for number one. They think they are the center of the universe and everyone and everything is there to make them happy. Scouts and success-minded people learn that it is really the other way around. If you look out for others first, if you help and serve others before yourself, you will be happier, more productive and live a better life.

LAUGH FREELY

One of the most valued qualities of friendship is the ability to laugh together. People love to have someone in their life who they can have fun with, laugh with and just flat-out enjoy. Yes, it is important to have a friend to walk through the difficult times with, but you do not, or should not, live in the difficult times. Even then, when you are stressed and facing challenges, nothing works better to relieve the stress than a good laugh. Be a friend that people can laugh with as well as cry with.

During a summer camp, I learned a very valuable lesson from the

Scouts I was with. I learned, once again, how to have fun. As with most of us who live through adulthood, I forgot what it was like to just sit around with friends and have a good laugh for no reason at all. I watched and the boys were joking and laughing and enjoying being together. Some may call that being silly, I saw it as the key to survival. It was like a refreshing dip in a pool and I am so grateful to be able to just laugh with friends again.

EXCEL IN LOYALTY

Friends are people who you depend on, to be honest, trustworthy and loyal. We need people in our lives that we know will never betray our trust or cause us harm. Those who think of themselves first cannot be loyal because loyalty is the very act of thinking of others, and what is best for them, over yourself. Be the person others know they can depend on to keep their secrets, support their dreams and be there when they need you.

I have been blessed in my life with several wonderful friends. These are friends I know I can always depend on and who I know will be there when I need them and I will do the same for them. I know of few things as valuable as a good friend. I hold to the words of the American author and philosopher, Henry David Thoreau (1817-1862), who said, "The most I can do for my friend is simply be his friend."

THE GROUP

There is a great balancing act that goes on in our world. On one hand, we need and desire to be one of the group. Teams can get more done than a person by themselves. We all have the need to be a part, to be accepted and to have others in our life. However, other times we can easily feel that we are just one of many. We do not feel anyone knows or cares about us as a person. All people need to know they are unique and special in some way, but to find this balance is not an easy task.

Scouting is designed in such a way that the Scout identifies with the group. He is a Boy Scout. One of an elite group of people who have embraced the Scout Oath and Law and who strive to be the best and do their duty. It is a wonderful and powerful group to be a part of. You will find Scouts all over the world and the thing they all have in common is the Scouting program.

At the same time, each Scout is an individual, they earn their ranks and badges on their own. They are encouraged to find and achieve their own purpose in life. Each possesses

"Scoutmasters deal with the individual boy rather than with the mass."

Sir Robert Baden-Powell
1857-1941
Founder of The Boy Scouts

their own set of skills and talents and are able to stand out and be their best at all times. The balance here is one that fulfills the needs of both the group and the individual without sacrificing one for the other.

You cannot change other people or make them think of things correctly. What you can do is change yourself and get your own thinking right. Success-minded people need to understand that they are indeed special. They have talents and strengths that make them uniquely equipped to fulfill their purpose. The danger here is the whole issue of pride because the fact that you are special does not mean you have more value than others.

The secret to real success is to understand that people are special and unique in their own way. There is no one else like them, or you, in the whole universe. Each has their own gifts and talents they bring to the group and into our lives.

We were not created as a group, when God in His great wisdom decided to put you on this planet, He looked at you as the individual, not as a group. God has no quota to fill and there is no one who is here by mistake. That means you can see others as special and worth caring for. People you meet have something to add to your life as you have something to add to theirs.

It is when we each see our value that we see the value of others. We are not competing with others for success; we are cheering each other on. We focus our energy on being the best we can be and helping others be the best they can be. When you succeed, I succeed and when I succeed you succeed. One of the best ways to discover the greatness in you is to help others discover the greatness in themselves.

This is the secret to making a group, whether it is a work team through a church, an organization, or work. Many times teams and groups fail in their mission because they want to hold onto that individual idea and do things their way. It is nothing more than a mass of individuals all fighting for control. There is no focus, no joint purpose, and no progress.

A team is a group of individual people who come together to share in a mission. That may be to work on a project, or perhaps to solve a problem, or even to change the world. Each individual person is willing to set their own personal agenda aside to work on the group agenda. They give their best to help the group succeed for they know when the group achieves its goal then they achieve their goal. As Apple founder, Steve Jobs (1955-2011) said, "Great things in business are never done by one person. They're done by a team of people."

Whether you are in Scouting, business, church or non-profit program, school or family, you need others to help you achieve the purpose and mission of the group. The key to making that group or team work is to understand that each member, is an individual and brings their own special skills and talents to the team. The success of the group depends on the willingness of each member to do their part and do their best. When combined, it is like baking a cake, you add all the ingredients and out comes a tasty treat.

Now, for an extra bonus on making a group/teams come together for the best of its ability. Make the members of this team all your friends and I do not mean to bring in your friends. In fact, sometimes the worse thing for a friendship is to work on a team together. I am talking about treating the members of the team as friends. Often, being on a team means that we spend a great deal of time with the other people on the team. Find out who they are and what they do, talk with them about things other than the work of the team. The closer the team is to friends the better their work will be. This friendship will make a greater desire for everyone to succeed. They will not be a competition, but rather a collaboration.

So how do you make this team friendly? By being the first to be friendly. I suggest you start off by being open and friendly right from the start. If people know you are there to help them succeed and that you truly care about them, and better yet, that you like them, they will, in turn, become friendly with you.

CHAPTER 7

BEING RESPECTFUL

(A Scout is Courteous)

"I seek constantly to improve my manners and graces, for they are the sugar to which all are attracted."

Og Mandino

1923-1996

Author

"A Scout is Courteous. A Scout is polite to people of all ages and positions. He understands that using good manners makes it easier for people to get along."

The Boy Scout Handbook

13ᵗʰ Edition

Most of us know the basics of saying "please" and "thank you," and not to talk with food in our mouths, opening the door for others or giving an elderly person our seat on the bus. Those are important and a sign of good manners, but true manners go much deeper. Manners, or if you will, courtesy, are shown in how we treat other people in both public and private life.

"It's the spirit within, not the veneer without, that makes a man."

Sir Robert Baden-Powell
1857-1941
Founder of The Boy Scouts

Manners are not a skill (although we do need to work on improving them) or talent, but a behavior. Because of that, no one can say they do not have the ability to show good manners or that rudeness is their natural talent. You do have control over your behavior. Remember God gave you control over only one thing in the entire universe and that is you. American businessman and former CEO of IBM, Thomas J. Watson (1874-1956) said, "Really big people are, above everything else, courteous, considerate and generous – not just to some people in some circumstances – but to everyone all the time."

The practice of good manners is the fifth point of the Scout Law. In my humble opinion, it is also the one paid the least attention to. I am not saying Scouts are rude. I know Scouts who are some of the politest people you will ever meet. However, I do think that Scouting, like our society in general, has fallen into the mindset that good manners are just not very important. Remember, rudeness is not the only result of bad manners. You can lack in proper manners and still not be directly rude to others. Rudeness is a behavior all on its own.

There was a time when practicing good manners was incorporated into our daily life. Children were taught good manners in both home and school. Not only did adults teach good manners to children, they practiced good manners themselves. Today we have developed a more casual society. I am not saying we need to go back to behavior in the 1800's, I like that we are more casual with each other today. However, the causality of this is that we started seeing good manners as old fashion and out dated and that is not at all true.

The basic practice of being polite is not a fashion to begin with. It is simply showing respect and kindness to others. Good manners are simple to do and make others feel you care about them. Scouting encourages young people to be respectful to others, and to treat everyone with dignity.

Ritz-Carlton's business motto is one of my favorites, "We are ladies and gentlemen serving ladies and gentlemen." Isn't that the best? I believe this should be the personal motto of anyone looking to have a successful life. It assumes two extremely important things. One is you are a lady or gentleman and if you believe yourself to be, so you will be. If you start behaving like a lady or gentleman, your whole perspective on the world around you changes. The second is you see others as ladies and gentlemen. When you start treating others as if they were, so shall they be, it is a wonderful win-win.

Good manners show others that you value them and respect them. It also shows others you have value and respect for yourself. Manners show confidence, discipline, and dependability. Think about it—don't you think higher of a person who shows good manners than one who is rude and thoughtless? Say you're a business professional looking for two candidates for a job, both with the same qualifications and experience. One has good manners, is properly dressed and positive. The other is slouching and looks like he has been dragged from under the bed and complaints. Who are you going to hire?

This does not mean that people with good manners have no fun or don't joke around. You can be the funniest guy in the room. Good manners doesn't mean you have to be straight-laced; it is just being courteous and polite to others. It reminds me of an A.A. Milne story, where Winnie the Pooh invites Tigger to his party.

Pooh: "Oh Tigger, where are your manners?"

Tigger: "I don't know, but I bet they're having more fun than I am."

Don't be deceived into thinking that being "selectively polite" is showing good manners. Nothing is ruder than a phony. You can pick a phony person out of a crowded room, they are the Eddie Haskell (for those old enough to remember 'Leave It to Beaver') of the group. They are polite and courteous to those who have influence or power over them, or from whom they can gain something. But when they are with family and friends, they become rude and unkind. Don't think they are not noticed, fake manners smell like old fish.

Fake manners tell people you cannot be trusted and that you are not truthful. It says you lack the integrity needed to move toward success. American Philosopher, Eric Hoffer (1898-1983) put it this way, "Rudeness is the weak man's imitation of strength."

True manners stand out every time. People are attracted to those who show good manners. We want to be around them, we go to them for help and refer them to others. Nothing will take you farther in the business world than good manners. Good manners breed a positive attitude and tell others that you can be trusted. When you hear gossip, you never hear someone being criticized for being too polite.

Developing good manners is not a difficult thing at all, it is just being aware of how you act toward others. As I said in the beginning, we all know the basics, you don't need to take a class or to read a dozen books. Yes, you can develop good manners into a career, which means you will need to learn the finer points of etiquette, but that is a different topic. For most of us, it is knowing how to be kind to others and showing our respect and appreciation for them.

Here are a few simple things to remember.

1. Always say "please" and "thank you."

2. Never talk unkindly of others or gossip.

3. Look for ways you can be helpful and kind to others.

4. Smile and look at people when you talk.

5. Shake hands and call people by name.

6. Remember, you are an example to others.

On the road to success in life, you will make many investments. Some will cost you dearly, but some of the most impactful, will cost you nothing. Good manners will be one of your most valuable assets and will do more for you professionally, socially and personally than anything else. Remember your manners.

> "Loyalty is a feature in a boy's character that inspires boundless hope."
> **Sir Robert Baden-Powell**
> **1857-1941**
> **Founder of The Boy Scouts**

As a people, we need to get over this idea that good manners are unimportant and of little use to us. We think if we say thank you to someone we have done a good thing. The lack of taking good manners seriously is the issue behind all the incivility we face in this country. We can see this lack of civility at the highest levels of government and business, and it is nothing more than the result of ignoring the importance of good manners.

In their 2009 book, The Cost of Bad Behavior, How Incivility is Damaging Your Business and What to Do About It, authors Christine Pearson and Christine Porath take an honest look at just what incivility is doing to our business and personal lives. They wrote;

"There should be little doubt that incivility has become a plague. It touches society across contexts, jumping like brush fires. You're offended by someone on the way to work and displace it by abruptly interrupting your assistant. An uncivil meeting in the morning sets you sniping at your waiter at lunch. What are the implications of such widespread incivility? For many people, the little rudenesses and gestures of disrespect that they encounter daily are so common as to go unnoticed. Yet, incivility in the workplace is noteworthy because of the enormous, unrecorded costs borne by organizations and their members. These costs hurt the economy and society as a whole."

The problem of incivility is like cancer in our society. There is no place where it is not causing damage or lasting harm. You can see it in the way we talk to each other. In the lack of respect given to those in authority or those who strive to do good. There are few areas of life (if any at all) that are not touched or many times slapped by the incivility of others.

Can you think of something that is not currently being criticized by someone? I cannot. The other day I was walking through the local grocery store and passed two ladies who were stocking the shelves. I could hear plainly their conversation about how the management was no good and they did not treat them fairly. They both wanted a different job. I thought to myself, "If they worked for me and acted this way in front of customers, they would have the freedom to find another job because they would not work for me any longer."

Incivility has grown to a critical mass in this country. In many ways it is due to the way leaders, in business, government and even in the church, treat each other and treat people in general. I will not leave the greater offender in this area out, the media. The news (so called) and entertainment media have been the greatest offender of incivility in the world. Daily people are fed with negative and worthless stories of people being offended by every little thing and who said what to whom. It is a cesspool of nonsense that is getting worse, not better.

Here is the important thing to remember. There is only one defense against this on slot of negativity and rudeness and it's good – old fashion – manners. I know it sounds far too simple for something this big, but it really is the only way. You cannot fight incivility with more incivility.

You have to show others what it is to be kind, civil and polite. The way to overcome rudeness is with manners and to ignore rude behavior altogether.

I said earlier that I felt the Scouts fell a bit too short on the Law of courteousness, and this is how. Good manners, which they are encouraged in Scouts, I do not see them taught often. Remember, we are working with young people who have had a little example of what good manners are all about. They do not see them on TV, or in movies or read about them in their books and sadly, many do not see them at home.

I realize there will not most likely be classes started in good manners, although we need them. Many adult people need these classes themselves. They would rather complain about the incivility in our nation than do something to make a difference. It is up to those who truly want to see us return to a more civil and polite people to do something.

Never be discouraged by impossible tasks and missions. I know that when we think of changes this big our whole society thinks it is beyond our abilities. I have always believed that if a goal is not impossible, it is too small. This my friends is impossible, but it can be done and has been before.

During the start of the 19th century in England, one of the most profitable enterprises was the slave trade. This was a moral outrage to many and yet impossible to stop. Too much power, money, and government to keep it going for anyone to stand against it, but someone did. His name was William Wilberforce (1759-1833). Wilberforce was a British member of parliament and the force behind the abolishment of the slave trade in England.

William Wilberforce said, "God Almighty has set before me two Great Objects, the suppression of the Slave Trade and the Reformation of Manners." These great objects were impossible to do, yet the task for Wilberforce was clear and without question as it is for us.

Incivility cannot go on as it has been or it will destroy all we hold dear and believe in. It will also destroy the thing we hold dearest, our children. Working together we can restore good manners and the dignity that is ours to claim. If our young is to learn good manners, they will have to learn it from us.

THE GOLDEN RULE IS GOLDEN

We are all familiar with the Golden Rule; we grew up being told that we should treat others, as we want to be treated. It is one of those sayings, like "you can grow up to be anything you want to be," but those telling us don't really believe it's true. The idea of treating others as we wish to be treated is a nice idea, but in this "me first" society we live in, it really does not work. Or does it?

The Golden Rule is also like any other truth, it is true whether you believe it or not. The fact is if you treat others as you wish to be treated, your life will be much happier and much easier. It works every time. Poet, Edwin Markham (1852-1940) said, "We have committed the Golden Rule to memory; let us now commit it to life." It is the only way to move it from a nice saying to a reality of life.

Scouts and success-minded people come to understand that this great truth works for your benefit or hurt, depending on how you use it. If you treat people well, they will treat you

> "The Good Turn will educate the boy out of the groove of selfishness."
> **Sir Robert Baden-Powell**
> **1857-1941**
> **Founder of The Boy Scouts**

well. If you treat them badly, then they treat you badly. When Jesus said this to His disciples, "Treat others the same way you want them to treat you." – Luke 6:31 NASB, He was not just telling them to play nice. He was stating an important universal principle. How you treat people will be how they treat you.

Author and speaker, Dr. John C. Maxwell wrote a book several years back called, There is No Such Thing as Business Ethics, a title that raises a lot of eyebrows. Maxwell's premise for the book is that there are only ethics. There is no division between business and personal ethics. He believes these ethics are based on the Golden Rule. Dr. Maxwell calls this practice, The Golden Zone and he writes, "The Golden Zone is a visible slice of life when someone is doing the good, the right, and the true with rhythm and regularity. Unlike the forest fire, the harvest of such a life is constant growth, life, and health. It is simply the zone when there is an ethical momentum." He went on to say, "The Golden Zone is where everyone seeks to be and do their best. It is the place where it is more about 'we' than 'me.' It is the place where young emerging players want to stay, and seasoned veterans don't want to leave."

So why would this "Golden Zone" be so attractive to people, especially professional people? Because when we live right and do what is right, we reap the rewards. Do you want to be treated with respect, kindness, and encouragement? Then treat others this way. No, not everyone will return the kindness, but enough that will make it worthwhile. Success-minded people know that the best way to get others to do what is good and right is for them to do what is good and right. "He does good to another," said Roman Philosopher Seneca (4 BC-65 AD), "does well to himself."

The Golden Rule is not a complicated or mysterious thing to follow. In fact, it is the easiest of all principles. You know how you like to be treated. You know what makes you feel good and what moves your forward. Just do unto others and you will understand why this rule is known as "Golden."

Scouts have applied this rule to many areas of Scouting, it is the foundation for doing a good turn daily. It is directly connected to all 12 points of the Scout Law. Scouts know that if they follow this Golden Rule, they will always come out on top. It is not always easy. We all, old and young, struggle with emotions and the desire to get even with those who hurt us, however, doing good, rather than, seeking revenge will never fail to give the best results.

The Golden Rule is also the foundation for all good manners. If this principle were followed, you would never see rudeness or incivility anywhere. Why? Because no one wants to be treated badly. We want people to treat us with respect and kindness. They want to know that when you do something for someone, no matter how small that some thing is, that it was appreciated.

WHAT OTHERS DESERVE

Now I will say something that will get me into trouble. If you want to see some of the worst manners on display, go to a restaurant on a Sunday and watch the after church crowd. Many will treat the wait staff like servants, leave bad tips and if they have heard a good message, they may put that bad tip in a track thinking it will bring the mistreated waitress/waiter to the light. I have seen this unfold far too many times to be accused of just picking on church people. Are we representing Christ or are we thinking of ourselves at that point? St. Francis of Assisi said, "Preach the Gospel at all times and when necessary use words." That means your action should speak louder than your words.

As a believer in Jesus Christ, I am saddened to see so many fellow believers treating those who serve them with disrespect. We are told to be the servants to all, even to those whose job it is to take care of us. Many in the service industry will tell you that Christians can be some of their hardest customers. Christians can be very demanding, expect much for little and forget to express our gratitude in words or deeds.

I do not mean to be picking on Christians; of course, this type of behavior is common among many in today's society. I do feel however that Christians should be the most polite people on the planet. After all, we were all treated far better than we deserve. We are all sinners and unworthy of forgiveness and love God has given to us through Christ Jesus. To follow the Golden rule, and the instructions of Christ, we should love others as He has loved us.

Success-minded people know things are always improved and people respond better to kindness and good manners. Those who serve us in our daily life should expect more from us than being able to fill our coffee cup. We are the only gospel many will see. If we are to change the world, as we have been commanded to do, we must do so by influence, not by demands. The English writer, Samuel Johnson (1709-1784) said, "He who has such little knowledge of human value as to seek happiness by changing anything, but his disposition will waste his life in fruitless efforts and multiply the grief he proposes to remove."

Scouts and success-minded people should show those around them, love, respect and recognition of the value people hold. If our Savior Jesus Christ was willing to give His life for the least of people, how can we treat anyone less than the precious treasure they are in the eyes of God? In the Scout Oath, a Scout promises to "help other people at all times," this means he will always be ready with a kind word, a thank you and show appreciation for all that is done for him.

Allow courtesy to be your calling card to the world around you and treat those who serve you with respect. Look them in the eye, smile, and thank them every time they serve you, even just filling your water glass. May we be such an example that restaurants everywhere will look forward to the

"In assisting his 'neighbour' every day to the best of his ability, and keeping truth, honesty, and kindness perpetually before him, the Boy Scout, with as little formality as possible, is pleasing God."

Sir Robert Baden-Powell
1857-1941
Founder of The Boy Scouts

after church crowd and welcome them with open arms. Remember, the words of the lady who wrote the book on good manners, Emily Post (1872-1960), who said, "Manners are a sensitive awareness of the feelings of others. If you have that awareness you have good manners, no matter which fork you use."

ALWAYS ROOM TO IMPROVE

When it comes to good manners, we all have a need for improvement. Manners are like any area of personal development, as long as you are alive, you can improve in some way. Good manners are about others more than they are about us. It is not if others have good manners, but how our manners affect those around us. Eighteenth Century Irish novelist, Laurence Sterne (1713-1768) said, "Respect for ourselves guides our morals; respect for others guides our manners." Good Manners show we respect others as valued people and that we treat all people kindly as well as equally.

Success-minded people also know that good manners will open more doors of opportunity than education or position ever will. English theologian, Richard Whately (1787-1863) said, "Manners are one of the greatest engines of influence ever given to man." Think about it, wouldn't you rather do business with a person of good manners and a positive attitude than with a rude grump? Most successful people would because people are attracted to a positive attitude and good manners. The late Author, Og Mandino (1923-1996) said, "I seek constantly to improve my manners and graces, for they are the sugar to which all are attracted."

In Scouting, we try to teach that there is more to good manners than just being nice to people. Good manners are a door of opportunity. As Scouts grow and get old enough to seek out a job, or if they are on a sports team, they find that being courteous and showing good sportsmanship will open many doors of opportunity for them. Good sportsmanship, a very important part of Scouting, is nothing more than good manners.

As I have said earlier, the development of good manners is not a hard thing or something that requires special training. It is simply respecting others, treating them as we wish to be treated and a bit of common sense. Everyone knows what rude is and everyone knows what good manners and kindness are. If you apply what you know, you will go a long way. If you do not do what you know is right, you will face the consequences. It is all up to you. Remember the wisdom from Lewis Carroll (1832-1898), author of Alice in Wonderland, "If you drink much from a bottle marked 'poison,' it is almost certain to disagree with you, sooner or later."

CHAPTER 8

BEING KIND

(A Scout is Kind)

"A happy boy is a good boy, a good boy is a good citizen."

William Hillcourt

1900-1992

Author of the Scoutmaster's Handbook

"A Scout is Kind. A Scout treats others as he wants to be treated. He knows there is strength in being gentle. He does not harm or kill any living thing without good reason."

The Boy Scout Handbook

13th Edition

I love living in an age of technology, computers, smart phones, Wi-Fi, and social media are all great tools. They allow us to talk and meet with people on the other side of the world. We have

"We must change boys from a 'what can I get' to a 'what can I give' attitude."
Sir Robert Baden-Powell
1857-1941
Founder of The Boy Scouts

more information readily available than Franklin, Edison or the Wright Brothers ever thought was possible. However, we must remember that with great freedom comes great responsibility. Just because you can say, anything to anyone in seconds does not mean you should. In the case of social media, usually you should not.

Scouts are taught a lot about technology and how to use it. They also take a course called, Cyber Chip, which from Cub Scouts to Boy Scouts, teaches them how to use the Internet and social media safely and properly. They know about cyber bullying, and what sites are not appropriate for them to go to. They are also taught about online manners.

Scouts, as well as success-minded people, understand the power of words. Words matter and try as you will, once said, you cannot take them back. Author, Napoleon Hill (1883-1970) said, "Think twice before you speak because your words and influences will plant the seed of either success or failure in the mind of another." This is true when it comes to social media. The words you write on Facebook, even if directed to only one person, are seen by hundreds of people.

I have seen people, who I know to be nice people, write some rude and nasty things about another or express negative and hurtful opinions on social media sites. I know these people would never be so rude to a person's face or do anything so embarrassing in public. Social media seems to make people think they are not seen or what they say and do just passes by the general public...this is untrue. As Sir Winston Churchill said, "We are masters of unsaid words, but slaves of those we let slip out."

As I have told Scouts several times, remember that when you hurt someone, even a friend, it does not go away. Many friendships have been destroyed by just a few careless words. The same is true about the pictures or memes you decide to post, they stay there. In times to come, when you do not even think about them anymore, they can come back to haunt you. The simple answer is, never post anything you will regret later.

We have all seen pictures that are suggestive or embarrassing posted on people's pages. I wrote a young friend of mine who posted a picture of himself and his girlfriend, "You do realize that your mother sees this?" Even more concerning, her father can see it. Why is it that something as simple as posting to your social media site can make our common sense fly out the window? The stories are endless of people who have gotten into trouble, lost their jobs or ruined relationships because of something they posted. The excuse for their action is mostly the same – "I wasn't thinking." In the words of the great William Shakespeare (1564-1616), "Words without thought never to heaven go."

In 2015, I published a Kindle Book titled, Oops! Did I really post that? Online Etiquette in the New Digital Age. This is a book on how to have online manners. I wrote the book because I was concerned about how many people were not only rude online, but were getting cruel. I am sorry to say that since that time, the problem has gotten worse. It is hard to believe so many people, good people, can be so nasty, cruel and vindictive. Social media could have been a love fest for families and friends, but it has become a hateful battleground for anyone who decides to vent.

The time has come to think and think hard, you are responsible for the things you say, whether in person or on social media. Success-minded people understand that social media is great for two things: 1) keeping in contact with friends and family and 2) building business relationships. Good manners dictate that you never use it to express opinions on politics, religion, or personal battles. Be encouraging and kind. You can talk about what you believe, but make it positive and helpful, not criticizing others who may disagree. The great French thinker, Blaise Pascal (1623-1662) said, "Kind words do not cost much. Yet they accomplish much."

I know this takes some thinking to do. I confess I too have entered into conversation on social media that really were not productive or encouraging. I have resolved to be one who encourages and strengthens others as best I can. It is a wonderful tool that when used positively can bless many. It can however, also hurt many if misused. Scottish Statesman, James Graham Montrose (1612-1650) gave some simple, yet powerful advice, "Never write what you dare not sign."

I believe in free speech, one of the greatest things about America is we can say what we think and not be worried about being pulled off to jail for it. I must say that this freedom is threatened many times, by what is known as political correctness, but for now, we still hold free speech dear. Former U.S. Senator and Supreme Court Justice, Hugo Black (1886-1971) said, "The Framers of the Constitution knew that free speech is the friend of change and revolution. But they also knew that it is always the deadliest enemy of tyranny."

Success-minded people, believing in the principle of free speech, know it is not good to say whatever you want, whenever you want to whomever you want. With freedom, comes great responsibility and the awareness that good manners override rude behavior. Some people tend to think that free speech gives them the right to be insulting and rude to others. Where I will be the first to say that there should never be laws against a person saying what they wish, I will say that common decency and civility should restrain a decent person from being deliberately hurtful.

For some reason, we have developed the idea that to stop bad behavior, you have to outlaw it. There are so many restrictions and laws now that our freedom as a people is in danger.

"The real way to gain happiness is to give it to others."
Sir Robert Baden-Powell
1857-1941
Founder of The Boy Scouts

Making laws against something is a slippery slope. Yes, there should be laws against things that put people in danger and cause harm to others. Stealing, murder, destruction of property, kidnapping and many other socially immoral acts, do need laws to protect others. However, you cannot pass laws against rudeness, that is an individuals responsibility and one that should be taught to every person and not tolerated in a proper society. Author, G.K. Chesterton (1874-1936) said, "We are justified in enforcing good morals, for they belong to all mankind; but we are not justified in enforcing good manners, for good manners always mean our own manners."

Success-minded people know there is no excuse for saying unkind things to others. Hurtful jokes and rude comments have no place in the life of a success-minded person, nor in the life and behavior of a Scout. As for those who do not care what they say and who they say it to, American Philosopher, Eric Hoffer (1898-1983) said, "Rudeness is the weak man's imitation of strength." Although rude people often think of themselves as clever, to those around them they appear as fools – and fools they are.

Scouts know that kindness demands that we think about how others will feel about what we say. There is never a need to be hurtful or unkind, you can be angry and upset, but you cannot be rude and unkind. When you are angry, when it comes to social media, silence is golden.

Always remember that the goal of the responsible speech is not to control what others say. Freedom of speech is something wonderful and we need to protect it. As George Washington said, "If the freedom of speech is taken away then dumb and silent we may be led, like sheep to the slaughter." Free speech is intended so we can speak our mind on things that matter and ideas that can change the world, not to tell off colored jokes or be insulting.

Let me say a word about political speech and social media. Chances are a Scout will not be making political remarks anyway. Most young people do not have a deep interest in the news and political events of the day, but when it comes to adults, look out. Social media is a good 80% political commentary and that commentary is not nice. I am a political person and love to discuss different ideas and comment on the happenings of our government. I have decided that I would not discuss politics in any form on social media.

For one thing, do you really think that someone's political thinking will change because you made your thought known? I not only doubt it, but I would almost guarantee it. However, the main reason I do not discuss politics on social media is that it brings out the very worst in people. There is so much needless hate and bitterness. No matter what side you may be on or how right you may feel, it is not good to breed that much hate. And that is what social media is, a breeding ground for hate.

We have many ways to effectively make our political feeling known. You can even run for office if you feel the need to do something. Get involved and express your freedoms as an American, just do something worth while, social media is not worth while. We all get angry from time to time and want to vent. I have on occasion slipped and commented on social media about some political issue I feel strongly about (I am not even near perfect). I can honestly say, not once did it change a thing and it always – always – made me regret it as soon as I posted it.

If social media can cause as much hate and disruption as it does, just think of the joy it could spread. If used properly, we could be encouraging readers to be their best. You could look at your social media in the morning and feel charged with all kinds of positive energy to face your day, rather than wanting to go back to bed and pull the covers over your head.

Try this, for one month; do not post anything that is political or negative in any way. Do not read anything that is political or negative in any way. See if you do not feel better, do better work and sleep better at night. Forget the pictures and comments with hate groups, victims of crime, terrorist atrocities, aborted babies and the like. Show us pictures of your baby, family picnics, grandchildren, even of your kittens, and puppies.

WE LIKE KIND PEOPLE

I guess you can say I am easily impressed. People impress me all the time. I take that back, I am impressed by things people do that are not so easy. Talent impresses me. No matter how it is shown, in the arts, skills, crafts or any personal expression, I am impressed by excellence. I love it when I see people, especially young people, strive for and exhibit excellence in what they do. That is one of the reasons I am so impressed with Scouts. They strive to do their best, and when we do our best we will encounter excellence. I will say most of all that I am impressed by honesty and kindness.

In my lifetime, I have had the great privilege to know some of the kindest and warmest people that have graced the planet. Yes, I know there are far more that I have not met, but I am more thankful for those I have met, than I am sorry for the ones I have not.

I think of a lady named Mary, I met her through a church I was attending at the time. Mary was in her late 50's and suffering from stage 4 cancer. Most of my encounters with Mary were in the hospital where she spent her last days. Mary was in great pain 90% of the time, yet she did not complain or even talk about it. All Mary wanted to do was encourage those who came to see her. She spent all her time talking about you, how you felt and what your dreams and hopes were in life.

I remember so clearly, always feeling good after visiting with Mary. My desire was to support and encourage her, yet I must confess that I was the one being encouraged. . One day, during a visit with Mary, I asked her if she felt my visits were of any help to her. I told her that she was such a blessing and help to me that I felt I was getting more than I was giving.

"Your visits are the best medicine I have", she said to me. "I know that by encouraging you, things will be better when I am gone. No one remembers a grump," she said, "I want to be remembered and I want to make a difference." And she got what she desired. It has been close to 40 years since I talked with Mary and she is still remembered, still loved and she did make a difference.

That is the thing about kind people they are remembered. Think about it, do you remember someone who was kind to you in your past? Most of us do and not only do we remember their name, but if we close our eyes we can still see their face. We do not tend to remember those who were unkind. As Mary said, "No one remembers a grump." Why do we want to? Kindness is the thing that makes the difference and that is a big difference in our lives.

I was impressed by a bunch of Scouts not too long ago. There were 13 adolescent boys camping for a week. Not once did we have to correct anyone, discipline or deal with bad behavior. They all did their part, worked well

"A fisherman does not bait his hook with food he likes. He uses food the fish likes. So with boys."

Sir Robert Baden-Powell
1857-1941
Founder of The Boy Scouts

together and had a lot of fun. The thing that impressed me, however, was how kind they were to each other. There was one Scout who had some emotional issues he was dealing with. He would keep to himself most of the time and always be the last as we walked anywhere. I saw these boys, without being told, treat him with kindness, wait for him and always do their best to include him in anything they did. This kind of kindness is rare in adults, let along young people. They were all real Scouts.

I believe kindness stands out because it is in such short supply. Kindness relates to good manners; however, it stands out from all others as a courteous act. Kindness is more than doing the right thing it is doing the best thing. It also goes far beyond just being nice to another person. Kindness touches every person and living thing on the planet. Kindness is universal and is always good and never selfish or self-serving.

EVERYTHING DESERVES KINDNESS

There are times when it seems like the whole world is hard and unkind. The people you pass on the street frown and look like they will bite your head off if you so much as whisper a "Good Morning." The news is full of stories of all the mean and nasty things people do to each other. No one has a kind word about anything or anyone. Is there no hope left in the world?

Now comes the Super Hero, the one who smiles at everyone with a nuclear smile that melts the hardest heart. This hero has the super power to do the kindest things with the ease of the preverbal hot knife through butter. While the people around them are mumbling, they - our Super Hero - are humming a happy tune and ready to win the day for goodness.

Okay, I admit I have gone a bit extreme here. However, there are times in this sad world that the person who is positive, kind and happy, seems like a long awaited super hero. That was what the Scouts on the camping trip were in my eyes, they did not wait for the day to be good, they made it good.

A positive mindset and a happy heart is nothing more than a choice we make every day. They are not gifts from on high or things we must study for and earn our "Heroes" degree. You just choose to be positive and kind to others. In fact, when you act kind and happy toward others, it builds on itself and you become stronger and stronger with each passing person.

The world needs as many heroes as it can get. It seems like things are going down the toilet, but the truth is there are many, many people who are happy, kind and do wonderful things for humanity. Be that hero and make a difference in the lives of every person you come in contact with. As the 19th century English critic, William Hazlitt (1778-1830) said, "A gentle word, a kind look, a good-natured smile, can work wonders and accomplish miracles." A lady I served in the Salvation Army with, when asked if she needed anything would always answer, "Just a smile and a few kind words." That is really all any of us need.

BEING KIND TO THE UNKIND

As with many things in life, being kind is always easier when the person you are dealing with is deserving of your kindness, or at least they appreciate you being kind. But how do you deal with a person who has no sense of kindness and does not appreciate anything done for them? We all know the type; these people are nasty, negative and downright unpleasant.

I remember my time working in customer service at a large museum here in Michigan. There were many great events throughout the year for both children and adults. I loved the children's events because kids were so excited and just wanted to have fun. The day was full of smiles, laughter, energy, and activity. I remember during an event with Thomas The Tank Engine, a boy of about 5 or 6 was bouncing up and down with excitement as Thomas came down the tracks. We had little problems when an event was focused on children.

The adults were another matter, it never failed that when the event was mainly adults, there were tons of complaints, yelling at our staff and all out rude behavior. They seemed to think every rule or policy was there just to keep them from doing what they wanted. It was always a challenge to deal with adults at a special event and never as much fun as the children were.

Of course, this does not represent all adults. In fact, the majority of people were pleasant and therefore a good time. But we all know that it only takes a few rude people to make any event go from a good time to a nightmare. I believe this is because the kind and well-mannered people go about their time and do not feel a need to make themselves known. Rude people feel they must make their presence and demands known to all.

Customer service is a great place to learn how to deal with people. It is a challenge to face an angry person and turn them into a happy customer. Each day as I went to work, that was my goal for the day. It took patience, courage and honest kindness on my part. The goal was to make each person who came to my office feel they were heard and their needs were important, not just to the company, but to me personally.

This challenge ended up working far better than I had hoped it would. Time and time again I found people who came to me angry, left me feeling good about their day. What I found was there were some basic steps to follow in dealing with unkind and unreasonable people. These steps are smile, listen, agree, and respect. I taught these steps to my staff and I have shared them with many others.

Again, allow me to be clear about something, in no way am I saying that all people who came to me with a problem were unkind and unpleasant? Many had a reasonable problem that was solvable. However, anyone who has worked in customer service or dealing with the public, know there are those who look for things to be angry about and they will always make themselves known.

Another important thing to remember is that it is not always the public that are the rude ones. I have dealt with some very unkind and unpleasant customer service and sales people. The steps I will share will work on both ends of the spectrum. The key is that you can show kindness to unkind people and see results.

SMILE.

There is no greater weapon in the arsenal of customer service than a good and sincere smile. There were times I could see the angry person coming toward my office and I knew I was going to be confronted. My first step was to greet them at the door with a smile and welcome them in. 99% of the time this move softened them up right away. They got the feeling, and it was a correct feeling, that they were talking with someone who wanted to help them. As a writer, Anthony J. D'Angelo said, "Smile, it is the key that fits the lock of everybody's heart."

In Scouting, (and we will deal more with the eighth point of the Scout Law, A Scout is Cheerful) Scouts learn that a good smile is a useful protection against conflict. Have you ever been around a really cheerful person? You soon feel that any problem can be worked out. It is hard to be mad at a person who has a smile on their face.

"It's the spirit within, not the veneer without, that makes a man."

Sir Robert Baden-Powell
1857-1941
Founder of The Boy Scouts

LISTEN.

Allow the person to express himself or herself. Look them in the eye and listen, do not comment and do not interrupt. Allow them to get it all out, even if they accuse you of things that are untrue or unpleasant. Believe me, I know this is not always easy. It is like allowing someone to throw up on you, but it will help. Just like throwing up, the person feels better when it is out of them. It also allows them to lose steam so they are more likely to listen to you when it is your turn to talk.

Scouting teaches that a true act of kindness is to listen – really listen – to others. Many times, people just want someone to hear them. Listening is an act of kindness that others can appreciate. Remember the quote by author and philosopher, Henry David Thoreau, "The greatest compliment that was ever paid me, was when one asked me what I thought, and attended to my answer."

Agree.

We all know the old adage, "The customer is always right." I honestly do not believe that to be true. In fact, I have found that many times the customer is not right at all. However, the customer is always "the customer" and we must them to believe they are right. Do not disqualify their complaint or insist you are right. It is not about you being right; it is about the customer being happy. Success-minded people face conflict ready to take responsibility, give no excuses and make it right. Unkind and unreasonable people are looking for something to fight about. Simply, do not give it to them.

Scouts know that in a conflict with others, it is more important to bring a resolution than it is to be proved to be right. So many disagreements come simply because someone must prove they are right. Scouts are taught that being right and doing the right thing can sometimes be two different things.

RESPECT.

Every person is owed our respect and I know it seems there are those who do not deserve our respect, however, they must be respected all the same. Success-minded people find that so many of the conflicts between people can be resolved simply by showing respect to each other. Respect is not agreement nor is it surrender. Respect is the willingness to recognize and accept our differences.

Scouting teaches to treat others as they wish to be treated. As mentioned when we talked about the Golden Rule, when we treat others in a way that we wish to be treated by them, we show the kindness we seek. Educator and author, P.M. Forni said in his book, Choosing Civility that, "Being civil means being constantly aware of others and weaving restraint, respect, and consideration into the very fabric of this awareness." Respect is being civil. Where there is no respect, you find no civility. A Scout is always civil and therefore always respectful.

Of course, as we all know too well, no matter how hard you try to be pleasant and helpful, you will always find those few who are simply unpleasant people. There is no way you can make them happy or satisfy their need to be unkind. What do you do in a case like this? The answer is easy to see, but not so easy to do. Be kind and accept that some people are just unkind by nature and do not take it personally.

It helps to remember that each of us is struggling through life. You do not know what the unkind person is dealing with or the type of day they had. Where this is no excuse for bad behavior, it is a reason. By remaining kind and respectful, you offer comfort and conviction to the person at the same time. Comfort in that you may be the only person they encounter that will not strike back or fight with them. Conviction because you become an example that it is possible to be kind and respectful no matter how badly you have been treated.

The greatest benefit, however, is what it will do to you. You can leave an unpleasant situation knowing you did your best and came out better from it. By being kind and respectful we make the world better. How? Because we are one less unkind person. I have always loved the words of Scottish philosopher and writer, Thomas Carlyle (1795-1881), who said, "Make yourself an honest man, and then you may be sure that there is one less scoundrel in the world."

ALL THINGS GREAT AND SMALL

We cannot have a discussion about kindness without bringing in the question of how we deal with the non-humans we share this planet with. In the Scout Handbook, A Scout is Kind and defined in part by saying, "He does not harm or kill any living thing without good reason." A Scout is kind to animals and cares for them as best he can.

Pets are a part of who we are as a people, they play an important role in our lives and for many of us, including me, they are part of our family. A Scout is taught to care and treat pets and other animals with kindness. They even have two merit badges, one in dog care and one in pet care. This does not include the badges they can earn in studying mammals, reptiles and more. The animal kingdom is not a foreign place to the Scout, but rather is something he comes to understand and respect.

I am a pet owner and have two dogs (we call them the boys) JoJo and Pip. They are very dear to us and we love having them in our lives. I have had a dog for most of my life. I loved each one and have missed each one who has passed on over the years. Here is the point I want to make, where I love and care for each of my dogs, they are dogs, not humans. I am not one who believes in giving human status to our pets. Yes, we love them and treat them with kindness and care, but they are not human and therefore they do not have the rights or abilities of human beings.

"True Scouts are the best friends of animals, for from living in the woods and wilds, and practising observation and tracking, they get to know more than other people about the ways and habits of birds and animals, and therefore they understand them and are more in sympathy with them."

Sir Robert Baden-Powell
1857-1941
Founder of The Boy Scouts

Having said this, we do have to be aware that these animals are dependent on us for care and protection. Dogs may have their ancestors among the wolves and coyotes, but most of them would be toast if tossed into the woods to fend for themselves. They have been bred and raised to be pets. They bring us great joy, but the responsibility to care and protect them is on us. People who cannot take their responsibility seriously should not be having pets in their home.

Not long ago I was working in my yard when I heard screaming. At first, I thought it was kids playing, but quickly realized it was a scream of panic. I ran out front to see a neighbor just a few doors down holding a large pit bull by the collar as it was shaking her little dog in its mouth.

I ran over and as I got to the porch the pit bull dropped the dog, the lady let go of the pit bull and went for her dog. Me, not thinking at the time, grabbed the pit bull by the collar - facing the dog – and held on. The pit bull took off, me still holding the collar, knocked me to the ground and dragged me about 20 feet before it sat down.

The next thing I know I was under the dog looking up at these massive jaws, still holding the collar. I also realized the dog was calm and did not intend to hurt me. A neighbor came over and held the dog so I could get up and we waited for the police to come. As I stood there holding on to the dog, I realized it really was a very nice dog. It was gentle, to humans anyway, and it just sat there with no trouble.

The owner of the pit bull lived across the street and he soon came over. By this time the police had arrived and it seems this had happened before. The problem was the owner did not keep the dog properly fenced in and it, along with another dog he owned, got out often. The dog was taken and put down. Where I do understand why this happened, I was saddened because it really was a very nice dog. The problem was not the dog, it was the owner who did not take care of his dogs.

One of the things a Scout is taught is that owning a dog, or any pet, is a responsibility. They are not a possession like a toy or a bike. They are living things that have feelings and needs and it is up to us to care for them. To neglect to care for a pet is a serious matter. No living thing should ever be mistreated or abused. Scouts know that the act of kindness includes all living things, whether they belong to you or not.

I have long believed that every boy should have a dog and every dog should have a boy. My grandson Dylan was with us when we got JoJo. Dylan and Jo were pups together. To this day, Jo is really Dylan's dog, all we have to do is tell Jo that "the boy" is coming over and he goes crazy. He loves Dylan and Dylan loves him. Dylan also knows that Jo needs care, kindness, and love in order to keep him healthy and strong. He understands all that and more.

CHAPTER 9

BEING LAW ABIDING

(A Scout is Obedient)

"Experience must be tempered with good judgment and a willingness to learn better ways of doing things."

The Boy Scouts of America Fieldbook

"A Scout is obedient. A Scout follows the rules of his family, school, and troop. He obeys the laws of his community and country. If he thinks these rules and laws are unfair, he seeks to have them changed in an orderly way."

The Boy Scout Handbook
13th Edition

I have always found it interesting that the harder we work at being different from everyone else, the more we are the same. I grew up in the 60's when the way we proved we were "nonconformist" was to conform to every other "non-conformist." Even

> "One of the first duties of a Scout is obedience to authority. He must obey his orders in the first place and put his own amusement or desires in the second."
> **Sir Robert Baden-Powell**
> **1857-1941**
> **Founder of The Boy Scouts**

today, people claim they are not part of the pack and are their own person, yet other than their name, you cannot tell them apart from the next guy.

There are those who really are different and unique and I like to refer to them as success-minded people. Rather than feeling they must prove their uniqueness by piercing every available part of their body, to taking rudeness to the level of an art, success-minded people work hard at being the best they can be. Success-minded people are people who believe that character, integrity and doing the right thing is always the best way to go. They understand that doing what is right and being truthful is not a case of following the crowd, but of individual choice. A choice they make with understanding and passion.

Somewhere in this crazy society we started to believe that to be angry, rude, self-centered and displaying bad behavior was somehow cool or fashionable. Success-minded people understand it is in doing right and standing for a right that we really become our own person. Anyone can exhibit a bad attitude or wrong behavior. As the late Corrie ten Boom (1892-1983) once said, "Any dead fish can float downstream."

Scouts are a different lot, yes, we all wear the same uniform, and follow the same principles for life, but when it comes to being individuals, you will not find two the same. Scouting encourages each Scout to discover his own talents and skills and to walk their own path. The biggest difference in a Scout is that they do not have to yell to the world, "Look! I am not like the rest." They are okay just being who they are. The world struggles to be different and be their own person, but a Scout just is.

It is time we make the decision to be different. We choose to stand out from the crowd and be the example, not the attraction. It takes courage and determination to be trustworthy, loyal, helpful, friendly, courteous, kind, obedient, cheerful, thrifty, brave, clean and reverent. These are not the qualities you see encouraged in our schools or government. It takes a person who can think for themselves and have the guts to stand alone if they must.

Never get defiance and rebellion confused with being an individual. A true individual is one who can follow the rules and still be themselves. They do not have to try to impress the world with how bad they are or how defiant they can be. They do what is right, not because they have to, but because it is the right thing to do. That takes courage and a person who knows who they are.

The lawless and rebellious are not different or unique at all. They are everywhere and can be found in any group of people. These are the ones who think that rules are not meant to be followed and they will do what they want with no concern who they hurt or step on. This takes no courage, no thought, and no individual thinking. These are the mindless masses who feel so empty and without identity that they have to cause hurt and damage just to feel noticed.

When you look at the truly successful people in this world, the ones who make a difference and stand out as unique in every way, they are the ones who make the least amount of waves in life. They live in peace and find happiness in what they do. They are not the parasite of society, living off everyone else, they are the ones who hold society together. They follow the rules and yet, stay on their own path. A path they created.

Scouts, as well as success-minded people, have understood for many years that doing what is right does not make you one of the many, it makes you a unique individual. These are the people who stand alone, these are the people who make a difference. These are the people who matter to the rest. The rebels need those who do what is right or they would not have any identity at all.

Rather than being the one who fights the rules of life, be the one who follows them. Not to flow with the group, but to do what is right. Not every law and rule are right and just, we all know that, but there is a right way to bring change. Defiance only brings confusion and does not cause change. Doing what is right, because it is right, always gets things, important things, done. As civil rights leader. Dr. Martin Luther King, Jr (1929-1968) said, "The time is always right to do what is right."

Be a different breed than the rest, be an example of what it means not to follow the crowd or to give up your ability to be you. Be positive, pleasant and encouraging to all you meet. They will take notice. As Mark Twain said, "Always do right. This will gratify some people and astonish the rest."

WHY WE HAVE RULES

I know it can be difficult to see or understand why we have rules and laws. For the young, it seems like an unnecessary restriction on our time and fun. As adults, we like rules as they apply to others, but in our own lives, we also find them unnecessary. However, rules and laws are the things that keep us, as a society, from going off the deep end. These rules and laws help regulate society, they protect us from harm and help us achieve our dreams without someone coming in and taking what is not theirs. The Judicial Learning Center defines it this way, "Laws are rules that bind all people living in a community. Laws protect our general safety, and ensure our rights as citizens against abuses by other people, by organizations, and by the government itself. We have laws to help provide for our general safety."

In Scouting, a Scout learns that following the rules is not restrictive, but rather the key to freedom and self-reliance. The rules in Scouting are there to keep people safe, give guidelines to achieve the best results in any task and to promote fun for everyone. It does not take a rocket scientist to see that it is the people who disregard rules and laws that cause problems, restrict freedom and lead to injury of both person and property. When the rules and laws are followed, we have order and safety and can live in peace with our neighbors.

> "There is no teaching to compare with example."
> **Sir Robert Baden-Powell**
> **1857-1941**
> **Founder of The Boy Scouts**

We live in a time when the rule of laws seems to be in question. Those who want things their way, not the right way threaten even the basic freedoms of our nation. Leaders at the highest levels of business, government, and religion compromise the rules and laws and seem to get away with it. This corruption and misbehavior have caused a tragic toll on our society as a whole.

Having said that, I do believe there are still good and honorable people in all levels of business, government, and religion who do not compromise what they know is good and right. Here too is an area that I love about Scouting. Scouts know that to be trustworthy and a person of honor; they must follow the rules – all the rules. Compromising what they know is right for the easy and profitable is never an option. Even if following the rules is inconvenient or costly, you do what is right because it is right.

This type of thinking always brings up the question, "What do you do if the rules are bad or need to be changed?" That is an important question and I will deal with it more in just a bit. For now, let's just say, there are rules for changing the rules.

The American way of life is based on a series of rules and laws. This is known as the U.S. Constitution and Bill of Rights. Here is the question you do not want to be asked, have you read them? Don't feel bad if the answer is no. The fact is few Americans have, with the exception of a few places of education (usually privet schools and colleges), the Constitution is seldom taught in our schools.

The Constitution and Bill of Rights are the founding documents of this great nation. To learn and understand them, you soon see why America is the leader of the free world. These rules and laws had constructed a society where freedom and liberty excel. They are designed in such a way that by following these rules and laws, one will not find restriction, but a greater personal freedom than anywhere in the world.

May I suggest you take the time to read both the Constitution and Bill of Rights? You can do it in a short amount of time. These are not mass volumes like many of the bills and regulations we have today. They are simple, clear and written for the common person to read and understand. They are easy to get, many times for free.

One of the best sources for, not only a free copy of the Constitution, but also a free course that will help explain it and its importance, is Hillsdale College based in Hillsdale, MI. It is part of the curriculum of the college that every student takes a course on the Constitution and now they offer it to the general public for free. Go to Hillsdale.edu for more information.

There are rules and laws that help guide us, not just on the national level. In fact, you have them at work, in school, in church and even in the home. At work, you may have an employee handbook that explains the policies of the company and what is expected of its employees. You also have a way to do your job. No matter what you do, there is a right way and a wrong way to do it. At school, you have expectations to fulfill and assessments to do. At church, you have a system in place that you follow in worship, and Bible study of ministry. This can change from church to church, but the thing they have in common is they do have a system. At home, every family has "house rules" of what is acceptable and what is not acceptable behavior in the family. No matter where you are, you will have rules and laws to follow.

The lessons Scouts learn as they progress in rank and earn merit badges will be helpful for them as they grow and pursue a career. They learn that these rules are not there just to give them something to do, but to help they achieve and do their very best. Many rules provide them with safety. How to chop wood, use a knife and build a fire are not projects Scouts are just tossed into. They must earn a card saying they have learned how to perform the tasks and the importance of safety involved. Even then, the Scout has a procedure to follow, which if violated could mean losing their card and having to relearn the lessons.

For example, for a Scout to use a knife or cut wood, they must earn what is called, Totin' Chip card. To do this the Scout must read and understand the safety rules in the Boy Scout Handbook. They have to demonstrate how to handle a knife, axe or saw. They learn how to respect property and not cause damage. They understand and can demonstrate how to set up and use an axe yard. Just to name a few of the things they need to know. Safety is always first and nothing is assumed.

So how does this apply to adults? It is nice to know the Scouts do things safely, but what about me in the workplace or at home? Adults have a very bad habit of thinking they know far more than they do. The idea of an adult going to all that bother to cut some wood seems absurd. However, these lessons are not just to keep the young safe, ask the guy who chopped into his foot or hit one of his children with a stray piece of wood. It happens all the time.

The importance of rules learned when we are young is that, if followed, we do not have to learn them again as we age. All Scouts, young and old, follow the rules when cutting wood or handling a knife, while at a Scout function. The fact is most follow them at home or away from

Scouts as well. Understanding that rules are there for a reason helps us make good decisions and do the right thing.

Later in life, we are more willing to follow the rules of the company, the rules for our skills and talents, and the rules for our family. These rules help us work at our best, do an excellent job at all we do and keep ourselves and others safe and happy.

Another way to see the usefulness of rules and how they work in our lives is to play a good game of Chess. Chess is a very popular game in Scouting and not by chance. Chess teaches that rules mean something and yet, rules do not stop a person from learning how to strategize and develop skill. Chess is a game that requires thinking, looking ahead and understanding your opponent. International Chess master, Gerry Kasparov put it this way, "Chess helps you concentrate, improve your logic. It teaches you to play by the rules and take responsibility for your actions, how to problem solve in an uncertain environment."

We encourage Scouts to play Chess at many Scouting activities and at home with family and friends. There is even a merit badge. I love to play Chess with my grandson (at this time he is a Star Scout). It helps us both sharpen our thinking and learn to solve problems. Chess is more than a game it is a learning experience.

One more reminder, the rules of life, on all levels is not just things made up on the spot so others can control us. The true rules for successful living have been around for as long as humankind has been on the planet. I love the words

> "If you make listening and observation your occupation you will gain much more than you can by talk."
> **Sir Robert Baden-Powell**
> **1857-1941**
> **Founder of The Boy Scouts**

of the great author and educator, Dale Carnegie (1888-1955), who said, "People who truly understand what is meant by self-reliance know they must live their lives by ethics rather than rules."

BREAKING THE RULES

How many times have you heard – or said – "Rules are made to be broken." It is a common idea and often used to show that the person is a rebel, defiant and self-made. Author Marcus Buckingham wrote the popular book, First, Break All The Rules. Other noted figures made statements encouraging that we break free from rules and do things our way.

Businessman, Richard Branson said, "You don't learn to walk by following rules. You learn by doing, and by falling over."

American General Douglas MacArthur said, "You are remembered for the rules you break."

Indian businessman, Vivek Wadhwa said, "A key ingredient in innovation is the ability to challenge authority and break rules."

Actress, Katharine Hepburn said, "If you obey all the rules you miss all the fun."

Actor, Dana Synder said, "The only rule is there's only one rule: no rules."

Where I agree with some of these statements and some I do not, I do believe they are all talking about the same thing. It is not the removal of all rules, as it may seem. Each of these people, whether in business, politics or the arts, has gained some success in what they do. Some, in fact, have achieved great success and they did that by following the rules.

What is being said is that you must be willing to think beyond what you know and do beyond what you have done. Rules that are to be broken are those restricting growth and development. We do face those every day. The worse is what is known as government regulations. These are rules set up by people with nothing to do, but make rules. They do not perform the tasks they regulate. They do not need to be creative or hard working to survive. These people make rules because it's their job.

Success-minded people need to understand that where rules are there to guide you, they are not there to stop you. That is the job of laws. The law that says one person cannot take what belongs to another person is there to protect your stuff and stop thieves from having their way. But the rule that said humans cannot fly, was not broken as much as it was just proven wrong by the Wright Brothers.

Rules may not be made to be broken, but they can be changed. A rule is based on what information is there at the time. Once people learn more and discover more, that information changes and so does the rule. When people do things just because that is how they always have done it, stop their creativity and growth.. They surrender to the current facts, rather than the belief that the facts can change.

One of the best examples of this in history is that of Thomas A. Edison. Edison believed that just because something was not done before, did not mean it could not be done. Edison was a prolific inventor holding 1,200 patents at the time of his death at age 84. Edison did not invent just to invent, he looked for things that people really needed. His inventions were useful, practical and changed our lives forever.

Here is the interesting thing about Thomas Edison; he was a man of rules. He understood the process of discovery and followed that process. He kept detailed notes of every success and every failure. That way if he needed to know what worked or did not work and why or how it worked or did not, he had it. Edison had a team of some of the most creative and brilliant minds in the world, and he had rules as to how things were to operate. Those rules, however, were not restrictive. Every person, including Edison, could seek out new discoveries and changes however they wished. It was how they handled those discoveries that fell under his rules.

Although Edison was famous for saying, "There are no rules here -- we're trying to accomplish something." That did not mean everyone did what they wanted. The key words to pull out here is not, "There are no rules here..." it is, "we're trying to accomplish something." The method, strategic planning and working do any advancement in science, education, medicine or even better living by the rules. The trick is remembering that there are no restrictions to what you can achieve or what can be done.

WHEN THE RULES ARE WRONG

Just as rules can be changed when new information is discovered, rules that are restrictive, oppressive and wrong can be changed to be better, opportunistic and freer. There are some rules, or laws, that cannot be changed, the Law of God, the Laws of nature, and the laws of success. These laws are just what they are. They are there for a purpose and, like them or not, they have not and do not change. You can ignore them, defy them or just refuse to follow them, but you cannot change them.

However, unlike the Ten Commandments, not all rules are written in stone. Rules and policies in the workplace, school, church and other organizations many times can and should be changed and updated. In many large and successful companies, rules and policies are changed all the time, even if the closest observer does not notice it. Change is a part of growth and if a business or any organization or even an individual person wishes to develop, change is a must.

Change, however, must be directed by wisdom. Change may be a natural part of the growth process, not all changes are for the best and not all are necessary. Change of any kind should be strategic and thought out. Here are a few rules to follow when you are looking at making changes:

1) Never change things for the sake of change. If there is no solid reason to change, don't.

2) Always change to make things better, easier or more effective. Rules and policies should not re-

"Happiness is within the reach of everyone, rich or poor. Yet comparatively few people are happy. I believe the reason for this is that the majority don't recognize happiness even when it is within their grasp."

Sir Robert Baden-Powell
1857-1941
Founder of The Boy Scouts

strict people from doing the best job they can do. Simple rule to follow: The best restrictions are the ones you take away.

3) Before making any changes in a policy or procedure, talk with those who it will affect the most. Get all the best input you can before changing things that may only make matters worse.

Let me be clear here, we are talking now about rules and policies, not laws. Changing a law is somewhat different and we will discuss this in a bit. Right now, let's look at those rules and policies we face daily and feel they need to be fixed. Keep in mind the words of the American poet, Maya Angelou (1928-2014), "If you don't like something, change it. If you can't change it, change your attitude."

The first question you need to ask is, "Is this rule wrong, or do I just disagree with it?" There is a big difference here. In Scouting, we teach Scouts that in life they will face many rules and policies they may not personally like. Kind of like, "eat your vegetables" or "go to bed early on school nights." The Scout understands there are many rules they face at home and in school that are not fun, or cramp their style or keeps them from having fun. What they mistakenly think is, "When I get older I will do whatever I want and no one will tell me what to do." For those of us who once held that belief, we have been thoroughly disappointed.

I remember when my oldest daughter Beth was a teenager. There were many rules of the house she was not in favor of. Her response to having to do things she did not want to do was always, "I can't wait till I am an adult!" Beth is now all grown up, married with six children of her own that she homeschools, and she and her husband own their own business. When the stress of life gets her frazzled, I love to ask, "So, how do you like being an adult?"

We notice this insistence on doing things their own way in young people quit often, however, do not forget they will learn this from you more than their friends. Adults often think that we do not have to follow the same rules in life as our children do simply because we are adults.

That is a mistake. We all have things we must do that we may not really want to do. I cannot tell you how many people on social media complain that they have to get up and go to work. The funny thing is when people think they can't wait till they can own their own business and work for themselves. They will go in when, and if, they feel like it. They will take great vacations and retire when they are forty. Those of us who do work for themselves find this very funny indeed.

Here is the reality of the entrepreneur, you have a dream. You invest all you have and then some into that dream. You work close to 24 hours a day 7 days a week, 52 weeks a year. You may get a vacation in 5 – 10 years if the business goes well. You work harder for yourself than you ever did for someone else. You are responsible. No excuses, no blaming others for things that go wrong. And no dumping the rules of good business just because they do not make you happy. So, I ask, "How do you like working for yourself?"

My point is this, we can find fault with anything and wish everything would change, however, it does not make it wrong. Rules are just that, rules. Life does not come with the ability to do whatever you want when you want it. At least it does not for responsible and reasonable people. Success-minded people learn that rules have a purpose and just because they can be inconvenient or uncomfortable, does not make them bad or wrong. You need to have a real and valid reason to change a rule.

There are several reasons to change a rule. One, Is the rule outdated and actually making things worse? Two, Is the rule keeping the company or a person from advancing and becoming better? Three, Is the rule ethically or morally wrong? Lets' look at each of these issues.

(The principles apply to business, educational organizations, churches medical, legal, and political organizations. Rather than list each one of these I will refer to them all, and any others that might apply, as organizations. Saving me a lot of time and you a lot of reading.)

Is the Rule Out of Date?

As I had said before, organizations and always growing and changing. Many times this can be faster than the policies and rules of the said organization. I have worked for businesses whose policies and rules have gone through massive changes, however, the employee handbook had not been updated in years. This can lead, not only to confusion of the employees, but to big and costly mistakes when they follow old policies and outdated procedures.

Every organization should review and update their handbooks, policies, and procedures each year to be sure that you and the staff are functioning on the same level. This is the perfect opportunity to look over the rules and policies of the company and see if they need to be changed or updated. Never accept the old, "But we have always done it this way" kind of thinking.

We live in rapidly changing times and if a company is to survive and grow, it has to be one that changes and becomes better. Nineteenth-century clergyman, William Pollard (1828-1893) wisely pointed out, "Without change, there is no innovation, creativity, or incentive for improvement. Those who initiate change will have a better opportunity to manage the change that is inevitable." And even one of today's top successful authors and trainers, Les Brown said, "You cannot expect to achieve new goals or move beyond your present circumstances unless you change."

When you review the rules and policies of your organization, ask yourself these three questions.

1) Does this apply to our organization today?

2) Does having this rule or policy make us better and safer or does it not do anything at all?

3) Why was this rule or policy added in the first place?

Never keep a rule or a policy that is useless, no longer applies or has no benefit to employees. The fewer rules there are, the better and happier everyone is in the end.

Is the Rule Holding the Organization or People back?

Rules must always do three things. 1) Instruct and guide in the most effective way to achieve a goal. 2) Keep the organization and people involved safe and free from harm. 3) Bring out the best in the organization, its people, and its value to the people it serves. If it is not achieving these goals, it is not helping your organization.

> "Life would pall if it were all sugar; salt is bitter if taken by itself; but when tasted as part of the dish, it savours the meat. Difficulties are the salt of life."
>
> **Sir Robert Baden-Powell**
> **1857-1941**
> **Founder of The Boy Scouts**

We have seen or worked for, organizations that use their rules and policies to control and dominate their people. They seem to have a fear of allowing those who work for them, the ability to do and be their best. These organizations would rather float with the status quo than allow their people to develop and grow beyond their control. It sounds crazy, but it happens all the time.

The only person who enjoys a dictatorship is the dictator, and that person is not having very much fun. Rules for the sake of control are useless and should be opposed. Rules should never be to stop people from being their best, but rather help them achieve that very goal. No one, not the person in charge, the organization or the person following the rule, gain anything from something that holds them back.

IS THE RULE ETHICALLY OR MORALLY WRONG?

No one should be expected, no matter your role in an organization or your loyalty to the organization, to do anything that is unethical or immoral. Ever! You will not find this kind of behavior listed in the employee manual or policy and procedures book, but you will find it in the culture of the organization itself.

In Scouting, we make sure all the Scouts understand that if they are ever asked to do anything that is unethical or immoral by any person, adult or youth, they are to refuse and report it to someone in authority.

It is a very serious matter and should not be dealt with lightly. The same applies when adults in the workplace or other areas of life face the same problem. The response is clear, simple and without question. Report it to someone in authority and flat-out refuse. No matter who is asking you and no matter what the reason may be for asking you.

CHANGING THE RULES

A good organization is one that is aware of its rules and policies and change them when needed. This leaves little in the way of staff complaining about the need for changes. However, even the best companies can have rules or policies they just don't notice because they only affect a very few. If you find a policy or rule that you truly believe needs to change or be updated, follow these simple steps.

1) Before you complain or request a meeting with a supervisor or leader, know what it is you are talking about. Sit down and write out why you believe the rule or policy is ineffective or wrong. Do you understand what is being asked of you? Why do you feel you cannot follow this rule? Have it in writing so your thoughts are clear and exact.

2) What will make it better? As you write out what you think is wrong with a rule, be sure to say how you can make it better. A complaint without a solution is of no use to a leader. They will welcome your idea for change as long as it is done as an idea for change and not a complaint.

3) Lastly, approach the issue with a positive attitude and one of making things better for all. Too many people want change, but cannot tell you what kind of change they want. Chances are better that you will be heard if you are positive and helpful than if you are complaining and disrespectful.

CHANGING THE LAW

It is one thing to change the rules of an organization, another to try to change the law of the land. Laws are not like policies that a group of leaders decide upon and put down in a book. Laws are formed through many difficult and complicated steps that I am neither prepared nor qualified to cover here. I do suggest that if you do not know how laws are formed, you should research it and learn more. Again, the Heritage Foundation is an excellent source for information.

What I do want to quickly discuss is how you can change or respond to an unfair or unjust law. Many of us have seen the judicial system in this country fail many times. We have laws that make no sense and others that are outright distrustful. I believe in the rule of law and support our system of government, however, when corruption and dishonesty start taking over our leaders, we are in trouble.

We often feel there is little we can do to change things. The idea of changing the government or even a law is beyond our abilities. Yet, every great transformation in the world started with one person who believed in something greater than himself. As the American scientist, Margaret Mead (1901-1978) said, "Never doubt that a small group of thoughtful, committed citizens can change the world; indeed, it's the only thing that ever has."

For those who want to make real change in the world they live in, may I pass on a few, not-so-simple things you can consider. Success-minded people know that when standing up for what is good and right because it is good and right, you will always find challenges. The difference is how we handle those challenges. In Scouting we want our young people to be willing to lisen, discuss and be open to change if needed. However, when it comes to standing for what is right, honest, good and moral we want them to see that backing down, compromise, and giving in to group pressure is never an option. So what do you do?

SEEK POLITICAL OFFICE

I start with this because it is the most unpopular. Again, the idea of running for office is far beyond what we believe we are capable of doing. However, this country was founded on the idea that the ordinary citizen could hold an office and have a say in the running of the country. It is a wonderful thing that we are seeing that happen again. Many ordinary citizens have stepped into the political arena and have won seats in local, state and federal government.

If you see change is needed, maybe you need to be that change. We are all familiar with the words of Irish statesman, Edmund Burke (1729-1797) "The only thing necessary for the triumph of evil is for good men to do nothing." We have seen this over and over again in both small things and big things, from company policies to government takeovers.

It seems too often when something unjust or unfair, or even outright wrong happens, the good people will rise up and complain, but no one does anything. Look at schools. We were

> "In Scouting you are combating the brooding of selfishness."
>
> **Sir Robert Baden-Powell**
> **1857-1941**
> **Founder of The Boy Scouts**

upset and bewildered when prayer was taken out of the classroom in 1962. We yelled and hollered and made a fuss, but few ran for election to the school boards or worked toward the department of education. We just tossed up our hands and walked away. Sadly, rather than filling our schools with a board of good Godly people, we abanded them to the more left-wing progressives and our schools have suffered greatly for it because good people did nothing.

If this sounds like a rebuke, I guess it is in a way. Not just to you, but also to me. There have been many things I saw that were wrong and did little to stop them. We cannot go back and change what is, but we can take a stand and change the future. If good and honest people, success-minded people, take their role in this country, we can again, in the words of our President, Donald Trump, "Make America Great again!"

GET INVOLVED – VOTE

I am happy to say that many success-minded people take the responsibility to vote seriously. Over the last few years, I know voting went down, but much of that was revived in the election of 2016. Voting is not just a way to get people into office, but it is our responsibility as Americans. Of all our many wonderful rights and privileges, voting is on top. So much so that if you do not practice this right, you have no right to complain about the outcome.

Getting involved is more than just showing up on election day and pulling a lever. Know your candidates, know what they believe and who they are today. If they stand for what is truthful, right and good, work to help them get elected. You can change your one vote to many by letting people know the truth.

Politics today is a nasty, wicked system of finding the worst about people and telling the world. Here is the truth, can any of us stand before the country and claim to be perfect? I surely can't, and I am sure you could not either It would not take a team of slimy reporters to find dirt on me. I have lots of it, but I can say this, I am not the person I was in high school. I am not who I was in my 20's. I have grown up, made right choices and truly done my best to honor my God in all I do. Do I fall short, sure, you do too! So why do we seek to find meaningless dirt on people who in the end can make things better?

Look at the person today, who are they and what have they done to make things better? If you find they are dishonest, disloyal, and corrupt, don't vote for them or support them. Do not let the nastiness of politics scare you away and do not become part of the nastiness. As president Trump said, "One of the key problems today is that politics is such a disgrace, good people don't go into government."

USE THE MARKETPLACE

Why is it that whenever there is something we oppose, we think of a boycott? As if our threats will change the immoral into moral and bad people into good. I see it all the time. Let's be honest, boycotts seldom, if ever work. One reason is we support a boycott that does not affect us personally. For example, let's say a store chain supports some political movement that you feel strongly against. It is bad and hurtful to us as a nation, therefore a boycott is called not to shop at that store. Here is the problem, you like that store and it is convenient for you. It is easy to think that your one sale will not make any difference. Convenience will always rule over boycott and the store knows it.

Making your feelings and opinions count is not difficult and can be very effective if you really want it to be. The free market is a wonderful thing. In this country, we have the freedom to get what we wish from who we wish. That is why we have such great competition. You can shop around and find what you want at the price you wish to pay.

If there is something you feel strongly about that a business is doing, then don't shop there, it is that easy. In time, as more and more people do not shop there, things will change or they go out of business. Currently, the media has been in the spotlight. We are given so many untrue stories and run around that the press is the least trusted element of our society. Here is the answer, stop buying the papers or watching the news. Find the sources you do trust and follow them.

Never understatement the power of the marketplace. It is a powerful tool and it is all yours. Without you, business, media, schools and such, it cannot survive. If enough good people make a stand, evil will always fall.

The rules and the laws can always change and be changed.

CHAPTER 10

BEING POSITIVE

(A Scout is Cheerful)

"It is the Scout's duty to be a sunshine-maker in the world."

The Boy Scout Handbook

1911

"A Scout is cheerful. A Scout looks for the bright side of life. He cheerfully does tasks that come his way and tries his best to make others happy, too."

The Boy Scout Handbook
13th Edition

"Positive thinking will let you do everything better than negative thinking will." So, said legendary author and motivational speaker, Zig Ziglar (1926-2012). This is one of the greatest truths you will discover in life. A positive and cheerful attitude will help you work better, have better relationships, feel closer to God and make your life the very best it can be. A positive and cheerful attitude cost nothing and is not a hidden secret to search out. It will open more doors of opportunity for you than all the education you could ever hope to have and is the best way to better pay, better health and better living.

"I believe that God put us in this jolly world to be happy and enjoy life."
Sir Robert Baden-Powell
1857-1941
Founder of The Boy Scouts

No matter what philosophy or method to achieve your dreams in life, you will always find a positive attitude at the top of the list. That is because it is an irreplaceable key to achievement, the eighth point of the Scout Law says that a Scout is cheerful. That is more than having the ability to laugh and have fun, (although that is part of it). To be cheerful, means you have a positive attitude about life and the tasks that you need to do to make it the very best.

Let's first understand some common misconceptions about positive thinking or attitudes. Positive thinkers are often thought of as people who lose touch with reality. They refuse to see anything negative and pretend that all is good and wonderful, no matter how bad things get. That is very far from the truth, in fact, positive people see life far more honestly than negative thinkers do. Positive people are the true realists of the human race.

Positive people see the world and life around them for exactly what it is. They know troubles and difficulties are all around us. They face the same challenges of work, home, and life like anyone else does. Here is the difference, positive people do not allow the difficulties of life to get them down and refuse to accept defeat.

There are a few things that the positive thinker has in his/her toolbox that negative thinkers do not. For one, positive thinkers know they are here on this planet for a purpose – and that purpose is good. They believe their Creator chose to create them to fulfill a specific part of His plan. They are not just a chance biological event, but rather a deliberate force. This belief gives one confidence, enthusiasm, and courage. After all, when you have the Creator of the universe behind you, how can you fail?

Another tool they hold is that life is all about learning. Positive people believe that as long as there is learning there is life. They see every person they meet, every event they face in the day as something to help them learn and grow. Therefore, the positive person does not have an ordinary day because each day is an event in itself. They face the new day with excitement and an expectation that something good is going to take place. It is hard not to be positive when you are always on the brink of a great discovery.

One more tool that a positive person relies on is knowing how to face problems and difficulties. In spite of what some may think, positive people, face many of the same difficulties that negative people do. The difference is negative people see a problem and allow it to overtake them. It is the old, "This kind of thing always happens to me" type of thinking. Negative people believe that if something is going to go wrong, it will for them. The interesting thing is, it usually does.

Positive people face problems knowing that there is a solution. They may not know it right away, but they do know that every problem has a solution. Their task is to find that solution and apply it. Here is the curious thing; they usually do find a solution to their problems.

Think about it, if negative thinkers believe the worse will always happen to them, and it does, and positive thinkers believe that they will always find the answer to problems, and they do, what is at work here. I am not a psychiatrist, philosopher or even a super smart person, but to me, it seems obvious, it is so because they make it so.

Our brain is an amazing thing, it is possible to plant a thought that is not even real, and the brain will make it real. It responds to what we put into it as well as what is around it. We all know someone (could even be yourself) who believes that people are out to get them. There is no physical reason for this belief, nor is there any reason to assume that people are out to get us. The only thing creating this fact is the thought on the part of the one believing it and believe me, that can be a powerful and very damaging belief.

It happens the same way for the negative thinker when it comes to the events of life. If you believe that nothing will work out for you, then everything that happens is greeted with a feeling of disappointment and dread. I have known many people who believe this very thing. No matter how great things may be, they are always wanting something more, or something different, or the timing is wrong, or it is too much work. The list of disappointments goes on and on. I get amazed at how they can come out on top and yet crawl right back to the bottom again.

Positive people, believe that everything in life is there for a reason. No matter what happens they can learn from it, grow because of it and add it to their list of experiences. They learn from mistakes, therefore, mistakes have a great purpose and are never a failure. They believe that difficulties can make them stronger and better, so they face the difficulties of life with the excitement of an athlete. They do not pretend the problems are not there, but they welcome them, rather than dread them.

Both positive and negative thinkers have a very different result, but they both use the very same methods to get there. They create in their thinking the results they end up with. It is a very deliberate choice on their part. No one does this for them, they are not the victims of any celestial plot, it is all their actions and theirs along.

Of all the tools in the positive thinker's tool box, this one is the big number one. It is the thing making all the difference in the world and the one that will never be taken from them. That tool is called gratitude. A positive person is a person who is grateful for their life and all the many blessings in it. Without a grateful heart, there is nothing left but the negative. I believe Melody Beattie, American author, said it best, "Gratitude makes sense of our past, brings peace for today, and creates a vision for tomorrow."

Here is a challenge for you, find a person who is really and truly grateful, who is also a negative thinker. I know you cannot because there is no such thing. Here is a better challenge, decide to be honestly grateful for the next 30 days and see if your life is not happier, more positive in every area and that those blessings do not increase. It is a strange thing, but when we are grateful for all we have, we end up with more. If we are not thankful for what we have, we lose what little we have.

In Scouts, we teach our young people to see all of life as a gift. Every tree, flower, and river, was created for them to enjoy. This not only builds a feeling of thankfulness for the wonders around them, but it also encourages them to care for these gifts and treat them with the respect and care they need to grow.

When a Scout is thankful he is also cheerful. It is almost impossible to be truly thankful and sad at the same time. Scouts should know that God created all things for their good and for that they should be exceedingly thankful. It is a fact, a grateful heart is a cheerful heart. The great thing is, it is all a choice and the choice is always ours to make.

PUT ON A HAPPY FACE

Sometimes happy people make you wonder. There are those people who are happy all the time, no matter what is going on in their life. What is up with that? Some may think that these people have a screw loose or that they do not face reality. The truth is, they really are the ones facing reality. They know that whether they are happy or sad, it is their choice and so they choose to be happy.

Facing the world with an attitude of happiness is not denying that bad things are happening. Happy people choose their attitude and take control of their lives. People whose moods change as the circumstances they face change, allow the world to control them. It is easy to feel bad and allow stress and sadness to control your life. You must be strong to be happy. Only those who believe that they have the power to control their feelings can face life with a song in their heart.

Scouts tend to be a pretty happy crowd; they follow the first rule of Scouting, which is to have fun. Whether they are swimming, playing a game, putting up a tent or cooking over an open fire, Scouts know how to have a good time. It's one of the things they do not have to be taught. It comes naturally to them. Humans were created to have fun and be cheerful. We are the ones who have broken that down and missed the mark.

So many people think that for an adult to have fun, means they are either doing something they should not be doing, are irresponsible, or are just plain crazy. Not one of those is true. Happy people are people who have learned how to live. It is not that weird to be able to love what you do, love your family, and your life. It is not abnormal to have fun. In the words of the great basketball champion, Michael Jorden, "Just play. Have fun. Enjoy the game."

How does one get this power? First, you must make the decision that you will not allow life to get you down. Happiness is not a fleeting emotion;

"A Scout smiles and whistles under all circumstances."
Sir Robert Baden-Powell
1857-1941
Founder of The Boy Scouts

it is always a decision we make. We are not happy that bad thing may happen, but happy in spite of it. When you choose to see the positive in life, you will be amazed at just how much positive there is to see. Life is full of adventure, discovery, and wonders that, when paid attention to, will thrill your heart.

Another way to enjoy a happy life it to act like it, keep a smile on your face. You will feel and act more pleasant if you simply stand up straight, look up and keep a smile on your face. Mark Twain once said, "If you keep smiling you will feel better and others will wonder what you are up to."

One secret to the happiness of a Scout is they purpose happiness. When you smile you cannot help but feel good. Try it. Keep smiling. Here is an experiment I did with some Scouts once and the results were great. I told them to stand up straight, look forward, put a great big smile on their face and try to think of something bad. What happened is the longer they did it, the more fun they had. They would look at each other with these big silly smiles on their faces and laugh. It became a big game and they had a lot of fun participating in it. The other thing that happened is they forgot to think of bad things, it never came into their minds that they were to think of something bad. They were having too much fun.

I know that all you sensible people reading this are thinking, "That is nice, but I cannot go around with a silly smile on my face all day. I have work to do." Granted, there are times when it may not exactly fit in, but what about right now. If you are in a room reading this with people about and you feel too self-conscience to start smiling, go into the bathroom or something. Just try it and you will see how it will do wonders for your attitude and outlook on things.

This may seem foolish to you, but it really is a serious matter. We are all under stress and face difficult times. The pressure of life can be a heavy weight you carry around with little hope of relief. You have a simple tool that can make the burden a bit lighter, the stress a bit less and can transform your state from one of weakness to strength. That tool is a smile, you can do this. If you are too controlled and dignified to do it, get others to do it. You will not be able to keep from joining in. There is nothing more contagious than a big silly smile, so spread it around.

I like to make a game of it. If I am in a crowd of people I will walk around and deliberately smile right at them. My goal is to see how many people smile back. I have discovered that the majority of people you smile at will smile back at you. Try this for yourself. Besides getting people to smile, it is just a lot of fun.

Always keep your thoughts positive and creative. Face each day as a new opportunity to succeed and move closer to your dreams. In short, happiness is in your control. Others cannot give it to you, nor can they take it away. Be happy just to be you. Share that happiness with others and you will see it grow. If you have the choice - and you do - choose to be happy. It's more fun!

JOY OF SERVICE

In 1960, American songwriter, Jule Styne (1905-1994) wrote the very popular song, Make Someone Happy. The song goes, "Make someone happy / Make just one someone happy / And you will be happy too." That simple truth slides by so many people. Look around you, how many people do you know who are not happy? Do you see friends and family, who are hurting, distressed, worried or discouraged? We live in difficult times and unhappiness has become a way of life for people.

The Scout Law states that a Scout is cheerful, meaning he smiles whenever he can. His obedience to orders is prompt and cheery. He never shirks nor grumbles at hardship. To be cheerful and positive is not living in an unreal world where you pretend that everything is okay. But rather the ability to stay positive in the midst of hardship and trial. It takes great strength and courage to be a cheerful person.

You now have an opportunity to become a hero. Make someone happy, that may seem like a big order, but it really is very simple. Here are a few ways you can spread some happiness wherever you go and make someone's life a bit better, not to mention you will enjoy it too.

SMILE AT EVERYONE

Nothing is easier than a smile. As you pass people on the street, in the office or store, give them a simple smile and move on. No need to talk or stop what you are doing, just smile. Those who are having a bad day will see that someone is happy. I am not saying their life will change just because you smiled at them, but you never know.

I am not talking about the big silly smile we talked about earlier. This is just a mild, warm, friendly smile that says you care. I have tried to make it a habit to smile at everyone I come in contact with. Some, many, will smile back, nothing is said, just a smile. Some will look at me like I know something they don't. And still, others will ignore me altogether and just walk past. Whatever the response, I feel good because I am the one smiling.

> "Fun, fighting, and feeding! These are the three indispensable elements of the boy's world."
> **Sir Robert Baden-Powell**
> **1857-1941**
> **Founder of The Boy Scouts**

SPEAK A FEW KIND WORDS

When you are standing with someone you never met, or waiting in line, smile at him or her and say something encouraging and kind. What I have often seen are people standing in line and one says to the other, "What is the problem that things are moving so slow?" That is not encouraging, all that does is spread the anger. Talk about things that are positive and uplifting.

Dr. John Maxwell talks about meeting people and in less than 30 seconds find something to compliment them on. Could be how they look, the fact that they seem happy, maybe it is how they respond to others. When you know what you are looking for, something to compliment them on, it is not that hard to find. It also can become somewhat of a game to see how good you can get at this.

Be Helpful and Enjoy It

Open a door for someone, help them with their packages, or allow them to step in front of you in line. The key is to do it with a smile and enjoy it. Little acts of kindness do so much to help lift the spirits of others and show them you care. None cost you anything and the rewards are endless. Simple acts of kindness are a wonderful way to spread a bit of happiness.

TV host, Oprah Winfrey had a whole segment on her talk show about doing random acts of kindness. It became a very popular idea for a while; people would go out of their way to do nice things for people. Winfrey said, "What I know for sure is that what you give comes back to you." And she was right. When you are kind to others, not just people you know, but perfect strangers, you will see kindness coming back to you.

This goes back to the Scout slogan of Do A Good Turn Daily. I guess you could say this was the Scout version of random acts of kindness, and they have been doing it a lot longer. Scouts have also discovered the secret that by showing kindness, you find real happiness. Not only do you make the person you have been kind to happy, but (as the song says) you make you happy too.

CHAPTER 11

BEING FRUGAL

(A Scout is Thrifty)

"Go light, and the lighter the better so that you have the simplest material for health comfort and enjoyment."

George W. Sears

1821-1870

Author

"A Scout is Thrifty. A Scout works to pay his way and to help others. He saves for the future. He protects and conserves natural resources. He is careful in his use of time, money, and property."

The Boy Scout Handbook
13th Edition

Here is one of the elements of the Scout Law that do not seem to fit into our current thinking as a society. It especially does not fit when talking to success-minded adults. If it read, A Scout Creates Wealth or A Scout Knows How to Attract Money, it might make sense to some. But thrifty? Never mind that we don't even use the word frugal anymore and for many, they do not even know what it means.

The act of being thrifty is one of the keys to attaining and keeping wealth. I am not talking about being selfish or miserly, but the ability to not waste things and how to properly handle money and possessions. Scouts are taught that people and things have value. The best way to have what you need is to care for what you have. Scouts are also taught that generosity is an important part of good character. However, how can you give what you do not have? Learning the importance of being thrifty allows us to have nice things, be in need of nothing and give to those we wish to share our blessings with.

One of the best examples we have of this principle is that of the great American Statesman, Benjamin Franklin (1706-1790). Franklin was an author, painter, inventor, politician, Ambassador and so much more. It was Franklin who invented bifocals, swim flippers, lightning rods and a cast iron wood heating stove named after him. All of which are in use today. Benjamin Franklin thought of and founded the public library, hospitals, insurance companies, the fire department and the U.S. Postal System. He is without question one of the greatest minds America has ever produced. The changes he made to the country and society as a whole affected and still fill our daily lives today.

One of the greatest impacts on society and the general public came in the form of a book. The autobiography of Benjamin Franklin, published in 1791 was far more than the story of his life. It was one of the first, personal development books published in this country. It was a how to book, on the best way to live a good and successful life. At one time it was required reading in schools across America, however today you find many students barely know who Benjamin Franklin was, let alone read his autobiography. I do strongly suggest that every parent and teacher of a person with access to young people, (that means you Scout leaders) encourage the reading of this book.

The most well-known part of this book is what is known as Franklin's 13 Virtues. This was a collection of, what started out as 12 behaviors that Benjamin Franklin believed would lead to a good and successful life. Later, Franklin added number 13, Humility to the list. He said it was the one thing he practiced, but could never get fully. As soon as he thought he had it, it showed he did not.

"Happiness doesn't come from being rich, nor merely from being successful in your career, nor by self-indulgence. One step towards happiness is to make yourself healthy and strong while you are a boy so that you can be useful and so you can enjoy life when you are a man."

Sir Robert Baden-Powell
1857-1941
Founder of The Boy Scouts

I want us to look at Franklins 13 virtues and see how they can apply and improve our lives. You will see a similarity between the 13 virtues and the 12 points of the Scout Law. That is because the elements of a good and successful life have not changed and still remain the same to this day. We may give them new names from time to time, but when you break them down, you see it is all the same. The list of virtues, Scout Law, the laws of success are all from the same principles of life, which you can take all the way back to the 10 commandments.

Here is the list of virtues. I have rewritten the definitions of each point right under the original so they are easier for many young people to understand. The way things are said today compared to the early eighteenth century, can create some unnecessary confusions among the readers.

BENJAMIN FRANKLIN'S 13 VIRTUES

1. Temperance: Eat not to dullness. Drink not to elevation. Self-Control: Do not over eat till you are stuffed. Do not get drunk.

2. Silence: Speak not but what may benefit others or yourself. Avoid trifling conversation.

Be Quiet: Only say things that will encourage and uplift others or yourself. Do not gossip or get involved in useless conversations.

3. Order: Let all your things have their places. Let each part of your business have its time. Be Organized: Keep your home, room and all areas of your life clean and orderly. Give the right amount of time for each thing you have to do, be it study, work, socializing or religious duties.

4. Resolution: Resolve to perform what you ought. Perform without fail what you resolve. Trustworthy: Do what you say you will do when you promise to do it. Be dependable.

5. Frugality: Make no expense but to do good to others or yourself. Waste nothing.Thrifty: Do not spend money on useless and worthless things. Save what you have so you can take care of yourself. Take care of your belongings.

6. Industry: Lose no time. Be always employed in something useful. Cut off all unnecessary actions. Work: Be useful to yourself and others. Have a productive job and do it well. Learn a skill or trade that will add value to the world you live in.

7. Sincerity: Use no hurtful deceit. Think innocently and justly; and if you speak, speak accordingly. Kindness: Do not hurt others with words or actions. Be kind to all people and living things. Be fair and just in all you do.

8. Justice: Wrong none by doing injuries, or omitting the benefits that are your duty. Honesty: Do not do anything underhanded or unethical. Do not steal, cheat or mislead anyone. Be a person other people can trust.

9. Moderation: Avoid extremes. Forbear resenting injuries so much as you think they deserve. Respect Limits: Do not overdo things. Always be your best and strive for excellence in what you do, however, never allow your efforts to excel to hurt or diminish someone else. If others hurt or diminish you, do not seek revenge or strike back.

10. Cleanliness: Tolerate no uncleanness in body, clothes, or habitation. Be Clean: Keep your body, mind, and spirit clean. Dress properly for each occupation and pick up after yourself. Keep your thoughts and language as clean as your body and living space.

11. Tranquility: Be not disturbed at trifles, or at accidents common or unavoidable. Cheerful: Do not allow the challenges and difficulties of the day to get you down or discouraged. Keep a positive attitude and be pleasant to everyone you meet.

12. Chastity: Rarely use venery but for health or offspring never to dullness, weakness, or the injury of your own or another's peace or reputation. Be Moral: Keep your behavior within the limits of morality. Do not be sexually active outside of the bonds of marriage. Keep away from pornography and other harmful elements.

13. Humility: Imitate Jesus and Socrates. Don't Be Prideful: Do not think of yourself as better than others. Live as a servant to others and help them on the way. Use the life of Christ as your road map.

> "Try and leave this world a little better than you found it, and when your turn comes to die, you can die happy in feeling that at any rate, you have not wasted your time but have done your best."
>
> **Sir Robert Baden-Powell**
> **1857-1941**
> **Founder of The Boy Scouts**

I know some of these may not seem relevant to our society and life today, however, these virtues are just as important today as they were in Franklin's time. Virtues are not thoughts and behaviors that change with the times. They are the very moral fiber of the things that make us good and right. In an article titled: The Virtuous Life by Brett & Kate McKay, The Art of Manliness, June 1, 2008, http://www.artofmanliness.com/2008/06/01/the-virtuous-life-wrap-up/, this excellent explanation of virtues is given.

"Today, "virtue" has taken on soft and effeminate connotations. But originally, the word "virtue" was inextricably connected to what it meant to be a true man. The word comes from the Latin virtus, which in turn is derived from vir, Latin for "manliness." These days' guys excuse their lack of virtue by hiding behind the excuse of being "just a guy." Men need to do better and strive to improve themselves each day. It's time to restore the tie between manliness and virtue."

Like the lack of importance the term virtue has acquired in recent time, so has the term thrifty. We live in a very affluent time where people think nothing of replacing things for even minor reasons. We will toss out a perfectly good piece of furniture, simply because we no longer like the color. The idea of mending clothes or repairing possessions around the house is almost unheard of. Why? Because we think it is just as easy to replace them.

RESPECT FOR THINGS

There is more to thrift than just saving money. Thrift is not so much about the lack of spending, as it is the lack of wasting. Scouts are taught that it is more important to take care of their equipment and belongings than it is to save for something new. There is a lesson in responsibility here that can transform a simple desire to save into a life lesson in personal management.

There are two key behaviors here that apply to both young and old. First is the care for personal belongings, this is to keep them in good repair and useful. The second is the care of property that does not belong to you. This can be things belonging to others, equipment and property belonging to a group or organization like a school, work or community, and open property like parks and woods.

It is a simple fact that when a person leaves his belongings in poor conditions or does not pick up and care for his own possessions, he will not be any more respectful of other peoples. It is not a lack of thriftiness causing someone not to take care of his or her things; it is a lack of responsibility. This lack of responsibility soon shows up in the workplace, in the home and personal appearance. They may say that it is a lack of caring about "things," as if our belongings are not important, but in fact it is irresponsible and laziness that is the problem.

Have you ever noticed people who seem to have very little, seldom take care of what they have? That is not by chance. It is not the lack of money or ability to replace what they have, it is that they do not understand you have to care for what you have before you can get something else. The same is true in reverse, those who take good care of what they have always seemed to have more.

Now, of course, I am not saying that people who have little are all lazy and those with plenty are all hard workers. If only life was that simple. We all know those who seem to have everything they could ever want and are as lazy as they come. We also know people who work hard and end up with very little. The point is not just things; it is the care of those things that are important.

Even if you can afford to buy new things every day of your life, if you do not care for what you have, you are irresponsible and lazy. Likewise, if you have little and yet care for your belongings, you are in a better place than those who can pay for something new.

Part of the teaching of the ninth point of the Scout Law, A Scout is Thrifty, is that a Scout takes care of things that do not belong to them as well as what does. Scouts spend a great deal of their time outdoors and in public areas. If you have been to a public park, water-front or camping area, you have noticed that many times trash is left on the ground, equipment like tables and toilet walls are carved up or written on. This is not the way of a Scout, and should not be the way of any success-minded person.

Scouts practice what is known as Leave No Trace. Simply put, the Scout leaves a place in better condition than they found it. There is no, "This is not my trash" and passing it buy. If a Scout sees trash on the ground he takes the responsibility to pick it up. The principles of Leave No Trace are followed every time a Scout, alone or with a group, go out camping, hiking or just to have some outdoor fun. Areas are clean and cared for, no property or plant life is destroyed or damaged. A Scout respects the area and leaves it in excellent shape for those who will use it later.

Scouts also follow what is called the Outdoor Code. It is learned and memorized along with the Scout Oath and Law. The Outdoor Code reads.

As an American, I will do my best to –

Be clean in my outdoor manners.

Be careful with fire.

Be considerate in the outdoors.

Be conservation-minded.

As with every point of the Scout Law, we have talked about, this does not just apply to boys in Scouts. Everyone of us must follow this example. It is easy to fuss and complain that the public parks are a mess, but it is another to actually do something about it. It becomes easy when everyone picks up after themselves.

"Nature study will show you how full of beautiful and wonderful things God has made the world for you to enjoy. Be contented with what you have got and make the best of it. Look on the bright side of things instead of the gloomy one."
Sir Robert Baden-Powell
1857-1941
Founder of The Boy Scouts

Good outdoor manners are not a complicated thing. By simply following the example of leaving an area better than you found it, we can keep our public areas pleasant to go to, save on taxes, which pay for them to be cared for and repaired, and we show ourselves responsible and caring as a citizen.

Let me add one more area where respect for things applies and that's in the use of other people's property. If you should borrow or have access to something that belongs to another, treat it with the care and respect that it deserves. Do not carelessly mistreat it or cause needless damage. If, through some mishap, the property is damaged or broken, replace it with something of equal value or above because once you borrow something you become responsible for its care.

LETTING OTHERS CARRY YOU

There are many reasons to save money. You may be saving so you can make a long-awaited purchase. You could be saving to take a trip or have a fun time with friends. The most important reason to save however, is simply to pay your own way.

In the Scout Handbook, they include in the definition of A Scout is Thrifty this statement. "Paying your own way with money you have earned gives you independence and pride. Even if you have only a few dollars, you have enough to save a bit for the future and even to share a bit with others."

This principle is even more important as we grow into adulthood. Being able to care for your own needs without the dependence of others or on the state is a source of self-esteem and pride. Those who have to depend on the kindness of others or what someone else thinks they should have ended up becoming are more than slaves to those sources. Someone else, not you, decided what you can have and what you cannot. Someone else, not you, decided where you can do and what you can have as your own. Humankind was not built to live in this way.

The key lesson here for both young people and adults is to have a proper appreciation for work. The ability to work and earn your own way has so many benefits in our lives. It helps us feel we are responsible for ourselves and that we are not dependent on someone or something else. It creates a sense of personal pride and satisfaction that is needed for a good life. We do not have to be earning tons of money to feel we are paying our own way. We only have to be responsible and not live outside our own resources.

I worked with a young man who learned this hard lesson years ago. He was a very ambitious fellow who for some time worked a couple of small jobs and earned enough to just barely get by. The opportunity came along for him to work at a job that offered him a real living. He took it and soon was making more than he had ever made in his life. This influx of cash was both a blessing and a curse at first.

As with so many who go from little to big, he got caught up in spending his money, rather than saving it. He bought new cars, watches and took trips he could not yet afford. To him, he had the money so he might as well spend it. His other problem was that he didn't have credit. He got into the thinking (as so many do) that he could afford the payments, so everything went on a credit card, or two, or three, or five.

Then, as the story often goes, the bottom fell out. Business took a turn down and just as quickly as he found his new position, he lost it. He also lost the flow of money that came from the position. Having no savings to fall back on, he could not make all the payments he had racked up. He lost the cars, the bank foreclosed on his house, the goodies had to be sold and bankruptcy soon followed.

Fortunately, he was the kind of person who learned from his mistakes. He did what he could to bring in enough to support himself and his family. Since he was ambushed and willing to work hard, it did not take him long before he found another opportunity even better than the first. He is now a successful businessman and doing very well for himself.

This time, however, he lives in a modest home he can afford. He drives good, used cars and lives within his means. He is also saving regularly so that if heaven forbid, a fall happens again, he is able to face it and not go under.

Learning how to handle money when you are young is important to our youth. By taking responsibility for our own needs and wants, we soon learn we can make our lives what we want them to be. It may take longer to pay cash for something, rather than go into debt, but you do have the assurance that it is yours and you will not have to lose it if things take a turn. Paying your own way is a great feeling and allows us to be in the driver's seat of our life.

In 1748, Benjamin Franklin wrote and published a pamphlet titled, Advice to a Young Tradesman, Written by an Old One. In this, he gives some sound advice on caring for yourself and handling money properly. It reads.

"In short, the way to wealth, if you desire it, is as plain as the way to market. It depends chiefly on two words, industry and frugality. Waste neither time nor money, but make the best use of both. He that gets all he can honestly, and saves all he gets (necessary expenses excepted) will certainly become rich."

American author, Thomas J. Stanley, wrote a very important book in 1995 titled, The Millionaire Next Door. In this book, he looks at the wealth and lifestyles of many Americans. The difference between the two groups was that one group lives lavish and luxurious lifestyles and other lived simple humble lives. His discovery was eye opening. Stanley found that those who lived in luxury were often in financial straights and deeply in debt. Those who live more simple and practical life-

> "It always seems to me so odd that when a man dies, he takes out with him all the knowledge that he has got in his lifetime whilst sowing his wild oats or winning successes. And he leaves his sons or younger brothers to go through all the work of learning it over again from their own experience."
>
> **Sir Robert Baden-Powell**
> **1857-1941**
> **Founder of The Boy Scouts**

styles tended to have great wealth. These are our neighbors, who do not seem to have great wealth, however, many times they really are the millionaire next door.

Thomas Stanley said, "Many people who live in expensive homes and drive luxury cars do not actually have much wealth. Then, we discovered something even odder. Many people who have a great deal of wealth do not even live in upscale neighborhoods." He went on to say, "Wealth is more often the result of a lifestyle of hard work, perseverance, planning, and, most of all, self-discipline."

If someone wishes to gain wealth they must first learn how to handle what they have. Wealth is of no use if you only intend to spend it. It is far easier to spend than it is to earn. Money does not just come to us. Praying to win the lottery or hoping some unknown relative will die and leave you a fortune is not facing reality. People become wealthy because they earn their wealth, they properly handle their wealth and save it.

THE ONE THING YOU CANNOT CONTROL

There is one thing you must pay attention to if you desire to become truly thrifty in your life. It is the most expensive resource you have and yet, one a person can fully possess and not have a dime to their name. You cannot save it, create more of it or even gain more of it. You can only use it wisely or waste it, that is all and it's called time.

Here is some great advice from businessman Lee Iacocca, "So what do we do? Anything. Something. So long as we just don't sit there. If we screw it up, start over. Try something else. If we wait until we're satisfied with all the uncertainties, it may be too late." Action requires a sense of urgency in order for it to be consistent. You need to know that you must do something to move forward. That is why we think big. When you have a big goal that is backed with passion and enthusiasm, then you are willing to get things done just to bring it about.

If you talk with a Scout about what they hope to achieve in their

Scouting life, you will hear big dreams. Not just to earn a few merit badges, but to earn all 137 of them. They do not just want to reach Eagle rank; they want to do it before they are 15 years old. They dream big because they are encouraged to dream big. They also understand that to achieve those big dreams they have to get to work, right now. Time will not stand still for anyone.

The old saying is, "There is no time like the present." The reality is, "There is no time but the present." Right now is all you have to work with because yesterday is gone. You can (and must) learn from it, but you cannot relive it. You cannot go back and correct mistakes or re-capture the victories. It is gone and past. Tomorrow is yet to come. You can (and must) plan for it, but you cannot give it ahead of its time. You do not fully know what it holds or how it will play out. Even the best-set plans for the future must be adjusted to unforeseen events. All you have is today for taking action, it is what you do now that matters. It is today that tells you if you learned from yesterday and if tomorrow is possible.

I hear many excuses on why people do not take action on their goals. I've heard them many times, and all are not based on reality. When you really look into them, you see they are covers for a lack of action. There is an old saying, "If you really want to do something, you'll find a way; if you don't you'll find an excuse." Excuses do not help you in any way. They do not advance you, solve your problems or show you answers. Excuses do nothing but set your time, destroy your dreams and make you lazy. As our old friend, Benjamin Franklin said, "He who is good at making excuses is good at very little else."

How many times have you waited for things to be right before you start taking action on something? We wait for the timing to be right, for more money, more education, more favorable economic conditions, for the job market to get better or any one of a million things. News flash!! Things will never get better than they are right now! Author, Napoleon Hill (1883-1970) said, "Don't wait. The time will never be just right."

Most of the things we wait to see improvements on are things that are out of our control. You cannot control time, the economy, the job market, other people, the weather or anything else. God in His perfect wisdom gave you the power to control only one thing in the entire universe, and that is you. You have the power to change you, to take action and achieve your dreams. You have the greatest power of all – the power of choice. Even God will not interfere with your power to choose.

Never base your destiny on things you cannot control or have no power to change. There will always be something standing in your way. There will always be someone telling you that you cannot do it, it is too impractical, wait for another day or you are just not good enough. Many times this comes from people who love us and care about us, but who are expressing their fears. However, you cannot change their fear. In the end, you must do what you know you have to do. It is your dream, your purpose and only you can make it happen or let it die. As tennis champion Arthur Ashe (1943-1993) said, "Start where you are. Use what you have. Do what you can."

Every person on this lovely planet is unique and different and we are all made differently, have different talents and skills, have different dreams and react to life in a different way. However, the one thing we all have in common is time. Each person who has ever lived or will live, has 60 seconds in a minute, 60 minutes in an hour, 24 hours in a day and 364 days in a year. No one gets more, and no one can save even one second of time. It really is a perfect system. As the great, Albert Einstein (1879-1955) said, "The only reason for time is so that everything doesn't happen at once."

It has never been about how much time we do or do not have. It is how we use our time that counts. Even more, it is that we do use our time. Every minute lost is gone forever. Author, poet and philosopher, Ralph Waldo Emerson (1803-1882) said, "Guard well your spare moments. They are like uncut diamonds. Discard them and their value will never be known. Improve them and they will become the brightest gems in a useful life." Time, like all precious things, must be used in order to benefit from its value.

The fear of not having time has caused many to rush into things and not take the time to be excellent. They see time as rushing by and think it is more important to get things done than to do them right. Coach John Wooden (1912-2012) rightly said, "If you don't have the time to do it right, when will you have time to do it over?" Never think you can control or save time by not using it wisely.

This principle that Coach Wooden taught are very important to teach young people. I have found that young people may hate doing a task such as, homework, cut the grass, clean up and the like, but they really hate having to do it over. In Scouting we help young people to understand that if they do their best the first time, they will not have to do things over. Each task, whether it be to set up camp or complete a merit badge, the Scout is told what needs to be done and what the finial expectation is. This way they know what they are trying to achieve as well as what needs to be done.

These lessons not only help the young person to do a task right the first time, but it helps instill the principle of doing their best as they grow into adults. If you think a young person hates to do a task over in order to do it right, tell an adult they have to. No one likes to redo their work. If we can learn this as young people, just think of the amount of time we save as adults.

"From the boys' point of view, scouting puts them into fraternity-gangs, which is their natural organisation, whether for games, mischief, or loafing; it gives them a smart dress and equipments; it appeals to their imagination and romance; and it engages them in an active, open-air life."
Sir Robert Baden-Powell
1857-1941
Founder of The Boy Scouts

I know of people who have a dream and they really would love to see it achieved. Their problem is that in order to do this, they need more education or they need to learn a new skill. They will have to go back to school for two to five years and the thought of being in school that long is too much for them to deal with. The fact is two to five years will pass in two to five years, no matter what they do. It is what is at the end of those two to five years that counts. It could be their dream or they could be in the same spot they are now.

"Today is the only time you have.," said Dr. John Maxwell, "It's too late for yesterday. And you can't depend on tomorrow." If you are to succeed in the achievement of your goal and if you are going to take, the action needed to go forward. It must be today. I love the words of Dawson Trotman, founder of the Navigators who said, "The greatest time waster is the time getting started." Time for action!

MAKE YOUR OWN MONEY

One of the yearly events in Scouting is business, the Scouts learn how to plan sales, make sales and benefit from sales. This wonderful and fearful activity is called POPCORN. Just like Girl Scouts have their world-famous cookies Boy Scouts have popcorn.

Popcorn sales have a few different purposes behind it. Some may be intended and some are just the results of the activity. For one, popcorn is the way a Scout pays their own way. They make a profit off the sales and it goes to their fees each year as well as toward camping. There are boys who have saved enough from fundraisers or who have families that can afford to pay these fees for them, however, that is discouraged. The point is to help the Scout earn his own way and not have to rely on others to pay for him.

Popcorn sales also go toward the Troop they are in. This will allow the Troop as a whole to pay their own way. It will buy needed equipment, awards and pay for some events. This practice of paying their own way, gives the scouts a sense of purpose and confidence to know they can achieve these goals on their own. That confidence helps them face the many other challenges they face in Scouting.

Another benefit of popcorn sales is it helps the Scout to better understand what it means to run your own business. Yes, they do this as a Troop; really they do this as an organization since the BSA as a whole does popcorn at the same time. But, as with many Scout activities, they also do it on their own. Each Scout has his orders to fill. He must get his material together, make his list of people he will sell to, take the orders, collect the money, fill the orders and turn the money in.

This is a lot to ask of a young person, however, I have seen the satisfaction of achieving something big by the Scouts. They know they did their part and, when popcorn time comes again, they are ready to go.

Remember this the next time someone you know who has a Scout talks to you about popcorn or you see the Scouts at your local grocery store. Buy some popcorn. Be a part of the free enterprise system because you will not only be helping Scouting with your money, you will be encouraging perhaps the next great businessman. You never know.

CHAPTER 12

BEING COURAGEOUS

(A Scout is Brave)

"Scouts experience life, rather than just studying life's possibilities."

Clarke Green

Author

"A Scout is brave. A Scout faces danger even if he is afraid. He does the right thing even when doing the wrong thing or doing nothing would be easier."

The Boy Scout Handbook

13th Edition

Fear may have many faces and may touch each of us in a different way, but it does touch each of us. We are not all afraid of the same things and we react differently to fear when we face it. The important thing to recognize is whatever the form or intensity, we all must deal with fear in our lives. No matter how brave you may seem to others, you will have to face fear. No matter how much you hope and pray that you will not have to deal with it, fear will come knocking on your door. It is a reality of life and is also something you can both control and overcome.

The American General, George S. Patton (1885-1945) said, "If we take the generally accepted definition of bravery as a quality, which knows no fear, I have never seen a brave man. All men are frightened. The more intelligent they are, the more they are frightened." There is no shame in fear, nor is their guilt, remorse or regret. Fear is a reality we all face. Now, the question is, what do we do with fear?

> "A week of camp life is worth six months of theoretical teaching in the meeting room."
> **Sir Robert Baden-Powell**
> **1857-1941**
> **Founder of The Boy Scouts**

Success-minded people know overcoming fear is not the removal of it from our lives. That is a futile battle. Overcoming fear is moving forward, achieving our goals and enjoying our success despite fear. It is controlling fear, rather than allowing fear to control us. As the great actor, John Wayne (1907-1979) once said, "Courage is being scared to death... and saddling up anyway." Success does not require the absence of fear, but it does require the development of courage.

One thing Scouts will tell you, is Scouting is not for the faint of heart. It can start off small, but over their Scouting career, boys face everything from the challengesof a fifty-mile hike to down right dangerous wilderness experiences. It may not seem like much to the adult looking in, but to a boy, some of their adventures are as intimidating as those faced by the great explorers of history. It takes courage to do what you have never done before. It takes courage to leave your comfort zone and face challenges that are unknown.

One of the places I have noticed is a challenge for Scouts to face the unknown, is summer camp. Now let me say, I love summer camp, it is a great experience for both the Scouts and the Scouters (adult Scouts). At the time of this writing, I have just got back from summer camp. I spent a week, living in tents in the woods with a group of adolescent boys, for some, it was their first time on an extended camping trip. Honestly, not once did the adult leaders have to correct or discipline anyone. They were fun to be with, kind and considerate to one another and helpful with everything.

Here is the challenge of summer camp for the new Scouts. You have boys between 11 and 18 years old. Some have never been camping and the few who have, this may be the longest they ever spent away from home. They are doing activities they never tried before, such as archery, gun shooting, rock climbing, swimming and boating as well as many other activities. Yes, this is really fun, but at the same time, it is new. That is the thing about fear; it does not have to be dangerous to cause uneasiness. The thing many fear more than danger is trying something new and failing in front of others.

Scouts, however, are taught to try new things and be willing to fail or goof up in order to learn and become their best. I use first-year campers here because once a Scout experiences summer camp it becomes the high point of his year. That is just how fear of new things goes. You may be uncomfortable at first, but once you experience it and it is no longer new, the fear goes away and you enjoy it. It is only those who allow the fear of new things keep them from the experience that never overcomes.

The challenge of facing something new does not go away after the first summer camp. Each year there are more new experiences and each presents a greater challenge. First-year Scouts may go on a five-mile hike. More experienced Scouts will face a 50-mile hike. What starts as a fun swim for the new Scout, later becomes a mile or two swim for the experienced Scout. There is always a greater challenge to face and a new experience to be had. By the time a boy leaves Scouting at age 18, he can have more experience with the outdoors and know more about taking care of his own survival, than many adults have in their whole lifetime.

Now, I want to talk to those who have been reading this thinking, "How brave do you have to be to be a kid at camp? I face scarier things than that every day. Good-Grief! It does not take much courage to camp out with a few of your buddies." I agree, you do face scarier things than this every day. The thing is, you also ignore, run away or hide from anything that pushes you out of your comfort zone. Scouts really have little choice, but to face their fears, adults, on the other hand, have the freedom to not deal with them at all.

Let me ask you this, how many opportunities have you missed simply because you did not feel comfortable or had the courage to jump into? If you are like most of us, and I believe you are, it has been many. Oh, we can cover it up by saying it was not in our plans or that we had more important things to do. The fact remains, we were not sure of the outcome and fear made us walk away.

I talk with people all the time who have allowed fear of the unknown and uncertainty of tomorrow, keep them from their dreams. It could be to start their own business or start a new career. It could mean going into a line of work that they have never done before, but have dreamed of since they were children. Whatever it may be fear has kept them trapped in the same place doing the same things.

The legendary radio host and author, Earl Nightengale (1921-1989) said, "All you need is the plan, the road map, and the courage to press onto your destination." "Oh, if life was that simple," you may say. Well get ready for a shock – it is, if you know what you want. If you know your purpose in life, and you take the time to create a plan on how to achieve that purpose, you are on your way. The problem comes in the next step, the step that many have allowed to keep them from fulfilling their purpose. That is the courage to press on until you achieve your goal.

The fulfillment of a goal is not for sissies. It takes courage to push away from the shore and head off to lands you have never been to before. The courage to do what you never thought you could do and step into the dark in order to see the light.

Walt Disney (1901-1966) was a man with a dream. He loved to draw and was taken by a new art form called animation. Disney faced failure after failure and rejection upon rejection, but he did not give up. This was what he wanted to do. It was what he believed he was created to do. Nothing else mattered, he just picked himself up and moved on.

His determination and courage not only allowed him to fulfill his dream of being a great animator, but he took the art of animation to places no one ever dreamed of before. He then did what all brave dreamers do, he started dreaming bigger and more impossible dreams. Today, everyone knows the name and story of Walt Disney and Disneyland and Disneyworld are visited by millions of people from all over the world.

"The Scoutmaster teaches boys to play the game by doing so himself."

Sir Robert Baden-Powell
1857-1941
Founder of The Boy Scouts

There is nothing impossible to the dreamer. If you overcome your fear and have the courage to do the impossible, you too can achieve that dream. Disney said, "All our dreams can come true if we have the courage to pursue them."

It takes courage to go after a dream. Everything you do, whether it is your first camp out or starting your own business, will require courage to get started and step out of that comfort zone, take risks and attack the unknown. You must be brave to start, to keep with it and to succeed. Only the brave take action and nothing happens without action.

HEROES ARE REAL

There are many ways to show courage and bravery that we all face. Going after your dreams is definitely one of them, however, it is not the only one. We, as adults, have access to one of, if not the best example of bravery there is. It can be shared and should be shared with our young as often as we can. That is the example of the military, the brave men and women who protect and serve this great nation of ours.

I believe in heroes, it is good to show our young, especially young boys, heroes they can look up to. For a long time, we have lost the importance of real heroes. America has suffered a heroic crisis, we have gone from a nation who promoted heroes to one that has abandoned them to the weaker elements of our society. Not long ago, the "good guy" was always the hero in movies, TV and even in the nightly news. Today we have developed a fractionation with the corrupt and evil characters in our entertainment and made them the focus of news and our education process.

Do you remember when it was cool to have a hero? Heroes were always honest, steady, kind but tough and they always won. Everyone wanted to be like the heroes. I am not talking about make believe superheroes like Superman, Batman or Wonder Woman, I mean the flesh and blood heroes like today's first responders, astronauts, soldiers, and sailors. Where have all the heroes gone? They are still there; it is us who got blinded by our age.

We are fortunate in Scouting to have many great heroes to use as examples. People like I mentioned at the start of this book, Ernest Thompson Seton, Secretary of State Rex Tillerson, Former Sectary of Defence, Robert Gates, Steve Fossett, Leo Thorsness, Neal Armstrong, and of course the founder of the Boy Scout movement, Sir Robert Baden-Powell (who was a well-known war hero before he founded the Scouts). The list of brave and notable Scouts goes on and on.

Scouting has influenced, changed and bettered our world. Scouts have been in every field and have achieved the impossible from flying around the world in a balloon, to walking on the moon. Our young people need these heroes in their lives. They need examples, how by following the Scout Law, they too can rise above the crowd and become a hero themselves. They need to know it is possible to be good and decent and win in this corrupt world. As the well-known writer, C.S. Lewis (1878-1963) said, "Since it is so likely that children will meet cruel enemies, let them at least have heard of brave knights and heroic courage."

What makes a hero? In their book, Raising Boys By Design, authors Juntz & Gurian give a wonderful, working definition of the word HERO.

Honor: Adhering to truth, values, compassion, and principles beyond self.

Enterprise: Working at important things, whether they seem small or large.

Responsibility: Carrying important people and things throughout life.

Originality: Being a dreamer, a thinker, and explorer of the world.

This is why I love applying the Scout Law to life. The principles are the elements that make up heroes. As we teach them to young people, it is not with the intent of making them better children, but making them better adults. The principles taught in the Scout Law are to be carried throughout life. Some former Scouts may have lost their way from time to time, however, there are many who practice and live by these principles every day.

Success-minded people need to get this clear, it is not the time to sit around and long for the days of heroes. It is the time to rise up and become heroes. It is up to us to be the heroes the world needs to get it through this very difficult time. We can no longer hope that someday, someone with courage and integrity will step up and make a stand. We must accept the responsibility to be that person. Just as the superheroes of old, when we see wrong, we need to make it right. When there is injustices and moral corruption, we need to take a stand. This could be in the political arena, the local school board or the organizations you belong to. The only heroes who will come save the day is you and me.

Yes, the mission is impossible and yes, it does look hopeless and we are far outnumbered. But isn't that the stuff that makes heroes? You do not need a hero to do the possible, only the impossible. You do not need a hero to correct mistakes; you need them to fight evil. Gregory L. Juntz & Michael Gurian also said, "Heroes have good character and strong self-discipline. These heroes are and can be our sons." from the book, Raising Boys By Design.

We need to be the heroes of today and teach our children to be the heroes of tomorrow. The thing is, there will always be evil in the world. There will be difficult times and impossible problems to face and there will always be the need for a hero.

I find it distressing that so often the true heroes of our day; first responders, our men and women in uniform and the police are represented in a negative fashion. Our young people were encouraged to see the police as heroes. They wanted to grow up to be people of courage, honesty and bring down the bad guys. Now, our sons and daughters look up to the bad guys.

"Football in itself is a grand game for developing a lad physically and also morally, for he learns to play with good temper and unselfishness, to play in his place and 'play the game,' and these are the best of training for any game of life."

Sir Robert Baden Powell
1857-1941
Founder of The Boy Scouts

Here is a reality that needs to be faced. Those in law-enforcement are the good guys and those who commit crimes are not. Dishonesty, hatred, violence against others and disregard of the law is always wrong.

This is where we have the big disconnect with reality. It is right and wrong in life and it is an absolute. Crime, lawbreaking in any way shape or form is wrong. To make it anything else is a lie and a disservice to our children.

Heroes come out of honor and respect and these qualities are taught, they do not just happen. When our children are taught in schools that the "Good Guys" are really "Bad Guys" and the "Bad Guys" are "Good Guys" it causes nothing but confusion. At one time it was the highlight of the school calendar to have the police come and talk to the class. This was an assembly the kids looked forward to. The police were seen as heroes of the community.

By-the-way, talks by the police and visits to the police station are still a part of Scouting. Scouts are taught to respect and honor those in our community that keep us safe and protect us from harm. Scouting also has Explorer groups of older Scouts that work directly with law enforcement to better understand and contribute to their service in the community.

I also see this in how we look at our military. It was not long ago when it was seen as an honor to be a part of any branch of the U.S. Military. Recruiters, who were once welcomed to our schools have since been banned. ROTC programs were a proud part of high schools across the country, and are now a thing of the past for most schools.

We have traded the importance of serving our country to safe spaces, denial of free speech in fear of offending someone and school-sanctioned protest against the police, military and those who fight and give their lives to protect us. This is what a lack of heroes has done to us. To re-quote author and educator, C.S. Lewis, "We make men without chests and expect from them virtue and enterprise. We laugh at honor and are shocked to find traitors in our midst."

Keep in mind that heroes are not just for the young, we all need, not only to recognize heroes in our midst, but to honor and respect them at all times. Support those you know who are serving or have served. Treat those in our communities who hold the responsibility to keep us safe and keep our laws in place with honor and respect. Be a person of good character and integrity so that you too may be a heroic example to others.

THE BULLIES OF LIFE

A topic covered often in Cub Scouts is bullying. We want the boys to know how to deal with bullies and not allow them to keep them down. It is also vital that we teach these young ones that being a bully is worse than facing one. No one likes a bully, no matter what your age.

As we get older we think the bullies in life go away, but I am sorry to say they do not, they just change form and tactics. Even in Boy Scouts, the issue of bullying is one of concern. As boys learn and follow the Scout Law, they understand that a Scout is helpful, friendly, courteous, kind, and cheerful, all the things that a bully is not. Where we see these qualities as honorable, Scouts know they will face the cowardly bullies, simply because the Scouts hold these values.

Success-minded people are all too familiar with the bullies of our age. They are the ones who try and stop you from achieving your goals. They can be in our family, workplace, church, government and among our friends. Adult bullies often hide behind a mask of concern, caring with a desire to "help," or even worse, they think they are protecting you. However, even though they disguise themselves, the end result is still the same, they discourage us from the achievement of our dreams and living as a person of good character.

People, young and older, who do their best, to be honest, dependable, and trustworthy are often referred to as being a "Boy Scout." Funny that people who say it think it is an insult. Success-minded people, as well as Scouts, take pride in knowing that people think of them in that way. If the fact that you can be trusted, have integrity, will not compromise and serve others, means you are acting like a Boy Scout, then you are doing things right.

These bullies, those who look down on good behavior and integrity, are so caught up in their foolishness they really do believe they are the right ones. They believe everyone should be just as corrupt and dishonest as they are. Those who live good and right lives are actual offenses to them. They hate all that is good and clean and will do all they can to bring down those who stand for truth and justices. Even the Bible talks about these people, if you read the first chapter of the letter to the Romans, where Paul talks about this kind of person. He writes in Romans 1:28-32.

28 And just as they did not see fit to acknowledge God any longer, God gave them over to a depraved mind, to do those things which are not proper, 29 being filled with all unrighteousness, wickedness, greed, evil; full of envy, murder, strife, deceit, malice; they are gossips, 30 slanderers, haters of God, insolent, arrogant, boastful, inventors of evil, disobedient to parents, 31 without understanding, untrustworthy, unloving, unmerciful; 32 and although they know the ordinance of God, that those who practice such things are worthy of death, they not only do the same but also give hearty approval to those who practice them.

This issue applies to Scouts as well as adults. All who choose to do what is good and right will have to deal with this type of person. Remember this, a bully does not have to be a stranger, bullies can be among our friends, co-workers, people we attend church with, our neighbors and even our family. A bully is anyone who mistreats you.

Let's look at a few ways these people can get into our lives, bully us and how we can effectively stand up to them.

THEY FILL US WITH NEGATIVITY.

These are the bullies that are always telling us what will not work and that you will always be a failure. Some say they are just looking

185

out for us, however, they are never encouraging or believing in what we do; just filling us with their negative thoughts.

"Scouting is a man's job cut down to a boy's size."
Sir Robert Baden-Powell
1857-1941
Founder of The Boy Scouts

The best way to deal with this bully is to remain positive and fill your mind and heart with positive things. In fact, when these bullies come around, you should be extremely positive and tell them how great life can be when you have a dream you believe in. Positivity repels these bullies like garlic to a vampire. They will walk away because they cannot stand being positive for too long.

THEY DISCOURAGE YOU FROM TAKING CHANCES.

Anyone who has had a dream and stepped out to achieve it, knows the person who is just waiting to tell you that it is too risky and you need to be careful. They try to fill you with fear of all the things that could go wrong. They always have a story of someone they know who ventured out and was destroyed by the desire of a dream.

Your greatest weapon is the dream you have, build on it and allow it to burn into a fire of passion. Remember, taking risks is the only way that success is ever achieved. Let the bullies know that you may indeed fail, however, if you do, you will get up and go for it again. As American scientist, Grace Hopper said, "A ship in port is safe, but that's not what ships are built for."

THEY WORK HARDER FOR OUR FAILURE THAN THEIR OWN SUCCESS.

Success-bullies have this strange drive to see us fail, in fact, they do more and work harder at seeing us fail or quit, than they will at achieving their own dreams. This is the saddest part about these bullies, they have no ability to encourage or see the best in others. The world is clouded by their own sense of failure.

Help these bullies see they too can be a success. Encourage them to believe in their dreams and let them know you believe in them as well. Encouragement, kindness and a truthful, "I believe in you" has changed many a bully into a successful person. It never hurts to try.

Everyone loves to see a bully put down. We love the movies when the little guy has had enough and stands up to the bully who then runs off crying. Scouting does not teach our Scouts to fight, it is discouraged and not tolerated in meetings or activities. However, Scouts are taught to be brave and to stand up to bullies. Scouts are not encouraged to fight, but they will not allow bullies to abuse them or those around them.

It is not the brave who need safe spaces, it is not the brave who get offended and demand others lose their rights to speak or go where they wish. It is not the brave who call names and accuse others, simply because they do not agree with them. That is what the bullies do. Bullies are cowards and are weak. Scouts and success-minded people are brave and strong.

TAKING A STAND

"Be sure you put your feet in the right place, then stand firm." So said the 16th President of the United States, Abraham Lincoln (1809-1865). Where it is always a fight to be brave, which is after all, what bravery is all about, it is the most difficult and most important when it means taking a stand for what is right.

One of the purposes of Scouting is teaching young people to be of good character. It teaches values, beliefs, and integrity. Scouting helps the Scout understand that what is right and good and true and Godly, do not change due to public opinion. They make up steadfast values that will remain true from youth to old age. People may change and society may change, but that which is right will always be right and that which is wrong will remain wrong.

We live in an ever-changing world and it does not take much to see that beliefs and opinions, especially those of our culture, change too. Some changes are not a case of going from right to wrong, they are simply social changes and are to be accepted, and at times, even encouraged. Take fashion for instance, we do not dress today as we did 100 years ago. In fact, we do not dress as we did 20 years ago. Music, styles in home and business, art and so much more are all in a constant state of change. However, when it comes to ethics, morals, and integrity, these things are steadfast. As another President, Thomas Jefferson (1743-1826), our 3rd President said, "In matters of style, swim with the current; in matters of principle, stand like a rock."

This reality was a given not too many years back, however, compromise and discretion have run amuck in our culture. Even a few of those who at one time were rocks for morality and ethics have given up the fight and accepted a lower form of life. When we cannot trust our leaders to do the right thing, it becomes confusing for the old as well as the young. Where is the line drawn? Who is it that can make a stand in an environment of compromise?

Despite the moral and ethical collapse of the culture we live in, there is hope for change back to the values and principles that made us great. This change will come as we better understand three very important tools at our disposal. These are knowing our anchors, sharing our knowledge, and exercising courage.

We are not the first to travel this road in life. Many good and Godly people have cut the path that is there for us to follow. They gave us the anchors that will keep us steady in stormy seas. These anchors are things like the Bible, the Laws of Nature, The Laws of Success, The Scout Law and the works of the great thinkers of the world. These things show us the way to do and how to deal with the troubles of our time.

The American Economist, John Kenneth Galbraith (1908-2006) said, "It is a far, far better thing to have a firm anchor in nonsense than to put out on the troubled seas of thought." These anchors will allow us to find the answers to moral and ethical challenges we face, however they will not protect us from the foolish and dangerous thinking of those around us.

Let us look at some of these anchors and the lessons they can give us.

THE BIBLE

The Bible is a guide on the right way to live out our lives and it shows us what God expects from us and, more importantly, what we can expect from God. It does not matter if you are a

> "The Scout Oath and Law are our binding disciplinary force."
> **Sir Robert Baden-Powell**
> **1857-1941**
> **Founder of The Boy Scouts**

believing Christian or not. Your beliefs do not change who God is and what He has said. That may seem narrow, and it is, because it was meant to be. I will explain this more as we talk about the 12th point of the Scout Law, A Scout is Reverent.

There are two important areas in the Bible that would be very helpful for a person seeking the moral and ethical anchor. First is the 10 Commandments, these Commandments are designed to give us a simple and solid guide to our relationship with God and with one another. Most of the laws in civil society are based on these 10 Commandments.

The second portion I would suggest you read is in the New Testament. Reading from the Book of Romans to the Book of Jude will give you all the information you need to live a successful and good/happy life. It is not a list of don'ts. I know people tend to see God's direction as telling you what you cannot do, however, that is never the case. God tells us what is best for us and all we can do to live a good, peaceable and successful life. Whether or not you choose to follow His direction is up to you. There are consequences to whatever you decide, the decision however is all yours.

LAWS OF NATURE

The universe is full of laws that we have come to call, the laws of nature. These include the force of gravity, the speed of light, the changing of the seasons, how plants grow and much more. Now, you may think it would take a real fool to believe they can avoid these laws and get away with it. You are right, but there are such people in the world.

There are people that have such a rebellious heart that they even fight the natural laws to do what they want. The sad fact is they always end up paying for it. Here is a law of nature that we all must recognize and accept and that's the law of consequence. There is a consequence to everything you do – everything. Sometimes those consequences are good and sometimes they are bad. The thing is, they are always there. American author, Alfred A. Montapert put it this way, "Every person has free choice. Free to obey or disobey the Natural Laws. Your choice determines the consequences."

No matter what the law is that you choose, you do have the freedom to reject it. There are those who say, "I do not want anyone or anything telling me what to do." That is your choice and you can do whatever you wish. Here is what is not your choice, the consequences. You can decide you do not wish to believe in the law of gravity. To show your defiance you go to the roof of your house and jump off, thinking you will float in the air. What will, not might or could happen, it will happen, you will hit the ground – hard. Falling to the ground is the consequence of disobeying the laws of gravity.

"But John," you may say, "no one is so stupid as to think they can defy the laws of gravity. That is ridiculous." Is it anymore ridicules to think you can lie, steal or cheat and not be found out? Is it any lesser ridiculous to think you can abuse your body and not suffer for it? People do ridiculous things all the time. That is because they fail to understand that all things, good or bad, have a consequence. Once you get that, you change the way you do things.

LAWS OF SUCCESS

The laws of success are a bit different in how they affect your life, not different in how they should be followed. I have studied success and personal development for many years. I have read and studied the greatest thinkers on these subjects. Franklin, Emerson, Hill, Carnegie, Ziglar, Robbins and the hundreds that came before and after them. You will find each one, in their own unique way, telling you the same things, even I use the same principles in my own writings.

I once had someone ask me why they should buy books dealing with success and personal development,if they all talk about the same principles. That is a good question, and it has a good answer. The principles of success are like the laws of nature. They do not change, no matter what the culture or place in history, and when followed, they work every time. The thing that does change is how we see and interpret these laws. Each person sees things a bit different and each person can speak to someone that the other writer cannot.

Do you have a favorite writer? Someone who speaks to you and you understand what they are saying? I hope so. Author and speaker, Jim Rohn (1930-2009) once said, "Pity the man who has a favorite restaurant, but not a favorite author." No matter what the genre of writing, fiction, not fiction, biographies or success, the basics of the content has many similar qualities. We can call these principles. However, the style and way the author reaches you will be different. This difference is what gets these principles to stick in your mind.

Some of the principles of success that you will find are these.

Have clearly defined goals.

Write goals and action plans down.

Take action right away.

Be positive.

Be kind and considerate to others.

Follow the Golden Rule.

Dream big.

When these steps are followed, they will result in the success of any venture. Just like the laws of nature, the laws of success have consequences. Follow them and you will reap good consequences, defy them and you will reap bad ones. It is always your choice.

THE SCOUT LAW

This I will spend less time on only because it is what this whole book is about. The Scout Law goes along with the laws of success. These are principles you cannot go wrong with. There is nothing in the Scout Law that anyone can say is not healthy or good for them. How can you go wrong by being trustworthy, loyal, helpful, friendly, courteous, kind, obedient, cheerful, thrifty, brave, clean or reverent?

That is one of the great things about Scouting. You get the young in something that can only teach them good things. Nothing in the Scout Law is there to cause harm or mislead someone. These 12 points are clean, simple to follow and all good.

WORKS OF GREAT THINKERS

We live in a truly amazing time in history, unlike any time before, we have access to all the great minds of the ages. With a simple click of a button, we can read almost everything that has ever been written. We can carry massive libraries in our pockets. The average person can read more and have access to more information than the most brilliant minds of the past. And yet, reading is at a real low in this country and to me, is even more unbelievable.

By now you have noticed I love to use quotes, that is because I do not feel I have to say something that was said better by people far more intelligent

"A boy can see the smoke rising from Sioux villages under the shadow of the Albert memorial."

Sir Robert Baden-Powell
1857-1941
Founder of The Boy Scouts

than I am. I collect quotes as somewhat of a hobby, I also love to read old books. Some of my greatest mentors have been men and women who died over 100 years before I was born. I cherish each one and go back to them for help time and time again.

My wife and I are avid readers, we have not been to any location in the world that we do not bring home more books. I also am an active reader, I write in my books, underline and keep notes. I do not borrow books because I will only write in them. I would rather buy a book I can take notes in and keep in my library for future use.

One of the Scout merit badges I love to counsel in is the reading badge. One of the joys of life is to introduce young people to the joy of reading. I remember, as a young person I, like so many, did not like to read. To me, reading was something you had to do for school. When I was about 15 years old I had a friend who introduced me to a book about the rulers of ancient Europe. I fell in love with history at the moment. I discovered that it wasn't I disliked reading, I disliked what I was reading. When I read books I want to love them.

I am not saying that all the writers, thinkers, philosophers and educators of old were always right. Some of the things they said were very wrong. However, if you use your values to help sort out the good from the not so good, you have much to learn from them. Let's face it, most of us are not on the level of Einstein, Lincoln, Franklin, Gallio or even many of today's thinkers. It is wisdom to learn from those who have much to teach us.

It takes a brave heart to develop true values and to have strength to stand for them. You will never know what to stand for if you are not open to learn and grow. Ignorance is never an excuse for wrong behavior. When we have solid values and beliefs, we also have courage. It is one thing to know that something is right, it is another to know why it is right. If you have not learned the foundations of your values, you will not be able to stand by them in the storms of life.

History will show you that all great leaders had these moral and ethical anchors in their lives. A great example of this from both sides is the difference between Sir Winston Churchill and Adolf Hitler during WWII. Hitler was a man driven by power and a desire to control the world. His lack of moral values alled the killing of millions of innocent people and the loss of freedom to many nations. Churchill on the other hand was a man of courage and a passion for freedom and the surivial of his nation. He was out numbered, out powered and saw great suffering of his people. Out of this he found courage to fight on and a determination to never give up. In the end, the courage and strength of the English people won the day. Hitler's life ended as he lead it, in shame and defeat. Churchill is remembered to this day for his courage to do want is right, no matter what the cost..

Those who seek to be leaders and agents for change in this world, are those who grab onto the anchors they are provided and stand firm. I love the work of the 40th President of the United States, Ronald Reagan (1911-2004), who said, "Evil is powerless if the good are unafraid."

CHIVALRY

We know that the fifth element of the Boy Scout Law is, A Scout is Courteous. To be courteous is more than just being able to say please and thank you at the right times. Being courteous is knowing how to treat others with respect and kindness, it is being able to show care for others and a willingness to go out of your way to be helpful. In short, it is to be a gentleman.

Some may think the concept of being a gentleman is outdated and no longer applies to our present-day society, but that is misguided thinking. The need for the real gentleman is more critical now than ever before. The shortage of gentleman is not a matter of culture or social norms; it is the fact we do not teach this principle to our boys anymore. They have few examples to follow and many times are taught that you must first look out for yourself - which is the opposite of being a real gentleman.

One of the best ways to look at being a gentleman is that of chivalry. The word chivalry congers up images of the Knights of the Round Table. And that is a good example. Knights of old were to be brave, kind, yet gentle with those who needed their aid. There is an amateur sporting team called, Knights of the Free Company. They have a great Facebook page where I found this quote, "Chivalry never dies. The gentleman in most men did. Being male is a matter of birth. Being a man is a matter of age. But, being a gentleman is a matter of choice."

Scouting strives to help young men learn that being a person of good manners and one who practices kindness to all, is a place of power, not weakness. There is no shame in being a gentleman. The shame comes from causing hurt and damage to others, when you can be a source of encouragement and kindness. Bravery is the very nature of the gentlemanly behavior. The weak and cowardly hide behind rudeness and cruelty.

So how do we restore this quality in our young people and return to a more civil and caring society? I do believe it is possible to change society by changing the people in it. We did not get to where we are by accident it was a deliberate choice. It will take a deliberate choice to change things for the better.

TEACH THE IMPORTANCE OF CARING

The key to good manners, acts of kindness and good behavior is nothing more than simply caring for and about other people. When we care about how others feel and how we can help them succeed, we cannot help but show good manners. It is the Golden Rule put into action, "Do to others as you would have them do to you." If we care, we will do what is right.

TEACH THE IMPORTANCE OF COURAGE

There are few men braver than a gentleman because it takes courage to do what is right. It is a brave man who will show respect and care for others. When you always show good manners and do what is right, some may criticize you and make fun of you. However, the real gentleman is willing to stand for what is right, help others and ignore the heat.

TEACH THE IMPORTANCE OF PRIDE

We tend to think that pride is an ego thing and something that must be avoided, but isn't the case. To take pride in yourself is to understand that touching the lives of others and how you behave matters. If you are proud of who you are and what you stand for, you will have confidence and willingness to do far more than what is expected of you. A gentleman is proud to be a servant to others, proud to be an American, and proud to be a Scout.

CHAPTER 13

BEING ORDERLY

(A Scout is Clean)

"Let the youth be taught to look for beauty in all he sees, to embody beauty in all he does, and the imagination will be both active and healthy."

Orison Swett Marden

1850-1924

Author/Publisher

"A Scout is clean. A Scout keeps his body and mind fit. He chooses friends who also live by high standards. He avoids profanity and pornography. He keeps his home and community clean."

The Boy Scout Handbook
13th Edition

One of my grandchildren's favorite games used to be dress up. My wife and I stocked up on Halloween costumes one year when they went on sale right after Halloween. Dress up is fun and good for the imagination, but what about when you really have to live the role you are going for? That is when the costume becomes a uniform and a uniform means business.

Uniforms come in all shapes and sizes and designs. For the business person, it can be a man or woman's suit, for the cook, it is their jacket and hat, for the first responder it would be the uniform of whatever department they

"The uniform makes for brotherhood, since when universally adopted it covers up all differences of class and country."
Sir Robert Baden-Powell
1857-1941
Founder of The Boy Scouts

were in. Uniforms help us know what a person does, they bring with them a degree of respect. When you see a person in uniform you know what they do and you expect certain behaviors from them.

In Scouting, we have two kinds of uniforms; one is called our class A uniform. That is the one most people are familiar with. When people see that uniform they know it is the Boy Scouts of America and they expect a certain behavior out of a Scout. The other is called our class B uniform and is often a T-shirt with the Troop logo on it or some other Scout related markings. Either way, it tells the world that you belong to Scouting and that you are a Scout.

Uniforms do something more as well, they make the person wearing them feel their job. When you are dressed to do work, no matter what the work is, you feel more confident and prepared. Your uniform gives you a feeling of authority and skill. People who dress for their job do better, feel better and look better. Those who wear anything they feel like to the office do not do their best. Studies have found that office workers, like students, who dress down, perform at a lower level than their fellow workers who dress in a professional manner.

I work from my home most of the time. As a writer, I am alone, except for the dogs, in my home office, sitting and banging on my computer keys. Still, before I start my day I am showered, shaved and dressed for work. I am not in a three-piece suite, but I do dress as I would if I was going to the office. Being dressed properly helps me feel like I am taking my work seriously. I stay focused and, even though I am home, I know I am working.

In Scouting, the guys always come to the Troop meeting in full class A uniforms. It helps them remember why they are there and that being a scout is more than just hanging out with the guys. It also gives them the feeling of belonging. Scouts wear their uniform with pride, just as any other person in uniform does.

We have seen that once dress codes were removed from schools, student's grade averages went down. When you dress to achieve, you do better than those who do not, it's a simple fact. Being dressed for the job we are doing affects us emotionally and physically. This is the reason standards are so high for those in the military, first responders, medical professionals and of course, Scouts.

Success-minded people know that to do their best, they must look their best. This does not mean you wear formal wear every day, but it does mean you are clean, neat and look professional. By taking the time and effort to look professional, you will feel better, people will treat you as a professional and you will have the confidence to be the best at what you do. It does not take a lot of work, but it has a whole lot of benefits.

WHEN LIFE IS A MESS

Where it is good to be dressed for work and look your best most of the time, the reality is, there are times when dirt is the order of the day. I may make sure that I am dressed for work when I am at my desk, but I am ready for dirt when I am in my garden. There is nothing better than getting my hands in the soil and ending a Saturday, dirty, sweaty and covered in mud.

Scouting can, and should often be a dirty experience as well. When you are hiking for 10 miles in the woods, you do not come out squicky clean. TV personality and host of Dirty Jobs, as well as an Eagle Scout, Mike Rowe, makes a great statement about Scouting when he said, "A scout is clean, but he is not afraid to get dirty."

When we talk about being clean, we are not saying that we should never get dirty. Dirt, from good work and good fun, is a great thing. I have always said when my grandchildren get dirty, and that is often, that dirt is important, things like plants and children grow in dirt. You will also find that hard work often means getting getting dirty. .

Getting dirty can make us feel like we have accomplished something. There is great satisfaction that comes after you have done a hard day's work. For many jobs, your work is one you know will be really dirty by the end of the day. These are good jobs that require skill, knowledge and a willingness to get dirty. I never want to give the impression that the only good jobs are office jobs.

Mike Rowe has become a voice for skilled labor and for work in general. I deeply appreciate his views that we must get back to the understanding of what a "good job" really is. Rowe said, "Dirt used to be a badge of honor. Dirt used to look like work. But we've scrubbed the dirt off the face of work, and consequently, we've created this suspicion of anything that's too dirty."

When we talk about being clean, we are looking at hygiene. A person can have proper hygiene and still get dirty, and these are two very different things. In fact, many people who have poor hygiene are not likely to get dirty from work. Poor hygiene comes from laziness and that does not fit the working person.

To be clean does not take a lot of work, taking a shower each day, brushing your teeth, putting on clean clothes and using deodorant, are not things that are difficult to do. It will not only make you feel good, but will be appreciated by those who are around you.

Keeping your body clean is only one part of what it means for a Scout to be clean. Your body is important, but it is not the only place you find dirt in your life. I have known many people who are neat and clean, well-dressed and yet live filthy lives. If we clean up our whole life we will be happier, more productive and healthier in all things. As Irish playwright, George Bernard Shaw (1856-1950) said, "Better keep yourself clean and bright; you are the window through which you must see the world."

> "Boys can see adventure in a dirty old duck puddle, and if the Scoutmaster is a boys' man he can see it, too."
> **Sir Robert Baden-Powell**
> **1857-1941**
> **Founder of The Boy Scouts**

MAKE YOUR BED

Part of "being clean" is keeping the space around you clean as well as your body. You can learn a great deal from how a person's living space looks and how they deal with life. I have seen people who look professional, clean and dressed well, but whose car is like a landfill on wheels. It is full of trash, smells bad and shows a passion for junk food. If you cannot keep your car clean, how can you be expected to be responsible for other areas of work, home, and life in general?

Earlier this year I read an excellent book that I recommend everyone read. It is a small book, but one of the most powerful I have read in a long time. The book is, Make Your Bed – Little things that can change your life...and maybe the world, by Admiral William H. McRaven. The book is his account of his years as a Navy Seal and the things he learned in that training. Admiral McRaven tells us, "If you want to change your life and maybe the world – start off by making your bed."

I have found that by making the bed first thing in the morning it gives me the feeling of having accomplished something right from the start. This motivates me to go on to the next thing and then it snowballs into a day of productivity and achievement.

Have you even had a day when you just can't seem to get started? Make your bed, it is easy to do and it gives some immediate satisfaction. Once the bed is made it stays that way till you return to it at night. And when you return, you find a nice neat, comfortable bed, rather than a messy nest that you have to sort through before you can get into it.

You will find that there are many things you can do to help you become more productive. Before you leave the house, clean up whatever dishes there might be. Put them in the dish washer or wash them up and put them away. This again, will help you feel you have achieved something and it will keep you from having to come home to a mess that will be waiting for you. The dish fairies will not come by and do them for you when you are gone. Dirty dishes are very patient; they will wait for you a whole week if they have to.

One of the things we do at Scout camp is inspect tents. Each morning the Scouts are expected to clean up their tents, put their things away where they belong and clean the grounds around their tents as well. Later that evening, recognition is given to the cleanest tents and camp sites. However, it is not the reward that inspires this exercise, it is the fact that they get busy at something first thing, and it keeps them productive all day. It is also a great life lesson on being responsible to take care of your things.

Keeping things clean and orderly is only a burden when they are not done. It is easy to pick-up after yourself. If you have trash by where you are sitting or in your car, simply get rid of it when you get out or walk away. Same as when you eat. It is not only a matter of cleanliness, but also of good manners to pick up your table setting and deal with it when you are done with a meal.

Really, of all the things we can do become a better person and have a better life, being clean Is the easiest. You just have to do it. No matter where you are, you will leave a mark and the better you are at cleaning up after yourself, the better that mark will be. As we talked about in the section on being thrifty, leave no trace. Not at home, at work, in the outdoors, or any place you happen to be.

Before we are done with this topic, I want to talk about a place that many have a hard time keeping neat and clean, that is your workspace. The old saying is, "A messy desk is the sign of an organized mind." That is not true, a messy desk is a messy desk. Piles of papers and different things actually cause us to be less productive and look awful. A clean desk that is well organized is one that will help you be more productive, do better work and simplify your projects.

Here is a system I learned from author and organizational expert, David Allen. Take a few hours to just work on your desk. Set all the piles in front of you and start from the top, taking it each piece of paper or folder at a time. Place it into four piles. One is what you can delegate to someone else. This can be a letter to answer, a project to complete or a task that someone else can do.

The second pile is for things that are to be filed. These can be projects that have been completed, information you need to hold on to, but do not need right now. The third pile is for things that you must see to yourself. These are letters, calls to make, projects to do that you have to attend yourself. The fourth and last pile is for things that are just pieces of paper. These can be old letters, information or notes, but have no use to you now and can be put in the trash.

Now that your sorting is done, go back through the piles and send out all the stuff that is to be delegated to the people who get it. Next, take the stack that is to be filed and do just that, file them. Note that if you can delegate the filing to someone else be sure that is what you do. Do not use your time doing things that others can do for you.

Next, go to the last stack, the trash pile and toss it out. That was easy! Now your desk is nice and neat and now all you have is one remaining pile. Before you start on that, I suggest you clean your office or cubical. A clean space will help you work better and now, back to the last stack. This is the work you have to do. Start at the top and work on each thing until it is done. If you have to wait till a particular time to do something, file it in a dated file so it is off your desk till you need it. When you complete it, move on to the next. You will find this the most productive way of getting your best work done.

This method will help you do what is important and get rid of what only bogs you down. When we have a mess before us all the time, you cannot focus on what you need to. Your mind is seeing everything at once, not one thing at a time. As David Allen, author of Getting Things Done, says, "You can do anything, but not everything."

> "When a boy finds someone who takes an interest in him, he responds and follows."
>
> **Sir Robert Baden-Powell**
> **1857-1941**
> **Founder of The Boy Scouts**

Scouts have a merit badge on Personal Management where they learn to organize their lives and how to get things done in a timely and organized manner. This lesson will be of great help to them as they get older and out into the work force. I believe organizational skills should be required to learn in high school. One of the issues we have in education is that students are told they have to study, but little time, if any, is given in teaching them how to study.

As you can see, keeping things clean has a bigger impact on our lives than we may think. The neat and well-organized person is a more productive and healthy person in all areas of life.

START ON THE INSIDE AND WORK OUT

Now, moving from the outside, let's move to cleanliness on the inside. To be honest, it really does need to be the other way around, however, I wanted to be able to focus on inner cleanliness so I moved it to the end of this chapter. Truth is, if you can keep the inside, your mind and soul clean, the rest is just a matter of details.

Let me give you an example. I was a 60's child. At 15 I left home and hitched-hiked across the US. My life was totally caught up in the hippie movement of the day. Drugs, sex and rock and roll was basically what I lived for. I had no real belief system other than that I was the center of the universe. I was selfish, dishonest, disrespectful and very much alone. I am not proud of the person I was and in the next chapter I go into more detail about how my life changed for the better. The point here is that all the negative in my life was not a result of the culture I lived in, my parents or my friends. The negative came from the inside. I was responsible for the wreck I had become at such a young age.

Living the way I did, meant I did not trust anyone and was afraid of everyone and everything. We have all seen people who are empty, lonely and unpleasant to be around. It is easy the think that you change their environment you will change their behavior. What you come to discover is that it is not an outside problem but an inside problem.

Think of your mind as a room, you can fill the room with treasures made up of all the finest things, or you can fill it with trash. Sometimes, it seems we have a mixture of both and the sad fact is, if you mix the two, eventually, the trash will take over. There is just too much trash available to us and not enough treasure. The treasure you have to look for and handle with care. Trash will find you and it doesn't care what you do with it or how you treat it, as long as it can stay with you.

"As a single footstep will not make a path on the earth, so a single thought will not make a pathway in the mind." Said author, Henry David Thoreau (1817-1862). "To make a deep physical path, we walk again and again. To make a deep mental path, we must think over and over the kind of thoughts we wish to dominate our lives." What you think about has a very powerful effect on your life. It will determine your attitude, your behavior and even your quality of life.

The person who thinks negative thoughts all the time will be depressed and down most of the time. The person who thinks about how others have done them wrong and been unfair to them, will be angry all the time. Likewise, the person who thinks about all the opportunities they have in life, will be enthusiastic about their day. The person who is grateful and thinks about all they have, will be positive and happy. It is simply a matter of what you focus on.

Jack Canfield, the author of the popular Chicken Soup for the Soul series, said, "Successful people maintain a positive focus in life no matter what is going on around them. They stay focused on their past successes rather than their past failures, and on the next action steps they need to take to get them closer to the fulfillment of their goals, rather than all the other distractions that life presents to them."

Success-minded people have discovered that the greatest strength you have is to control your thoughts. It takes deliberate effort to do this, however, without that effort, you will not only lose control of your thought-life, you will lose control of your life. No one can succeed in life if they do not have the power over their mind. As baseball Hall of Famer, Wade Boggs said, "A positive attitude causes a chain reaction of positive thoughts, events, and outcomes. It is a catalyst and it sparks extraordinary results."

When it comes to cleanliness, your mind can be your greatest protection against unethical and immoral behavior or your greatest enemy. Here is where what you put in your mind really matters. Those who dwell on thoughts of lust, injustice or dishonesty will in time allow these things to manifest themselves into reality. This is the destructive power of pornography, bloody and violent movies and negative images of all kinds.

People get the idea that just because something is in your head that no one else knows your secret and therefore it is safe from causing you any harm, but that is just not true. It does cause great harm to you and to how you respond to those in your life. I am not saying that if you look at pornography you will become a rapist (could happen, however), but I am saying that it will interfere with your thinking of those who you are in contact with every day. Lust is like cancer, it grows and grows, until it controls all you think about and all you do.

One of the things we do not talk a lot about in Scouts is sex. It's really a conversation for parents and religious leaders to have with the Scouts. However, that does not mean we ignore it either. A Scout is clean in his body, mind, speech, and behavior. Scouts are encouraged to keep their talk and action clean and under control. It does not take a class to teach right behavior to a Scout or any young person. They do know right from wrong.

Granted, the Scouts of today face some stronger moral challenges than they may have in the past. Society has told them that whatever they wish to do is okay, as long as it does not hurt anyone. What society does not tell them is that immoral behavior will always hurt them. The things they have access to can be very dangerous to their mind and soul. People can brush this aside as old fashion or prudish, but the fact remains, there are scores of young people whose lives have been ruined due to a lack of moral control.

Looking back at the story I just shared with you about my younger days. Understand this, just before I took off to discover the great unknown, I had been a Scout. I knew full well the value of the Scout Oath and Law. I knew what I was doing was against all I had been taught and believed. However, I was also told that freedom meant not living by any rules and doing whatever I thought was good for me. I was young, foolish and too self-centered for my own good. What I thought was freedom as soon a prison for me. I did indeed do what I wanted to do and I paid the price for it. That part of the story they never tell you.

You will find too often, the majority will approve something that has been seen as wrong for many years. In cases of custom, fashion, and lifestyle, this can not only be acceptable, but also needed. However, in matters of morality and ethics, it does not change from bad to good. The great Russin novelist, Loe Tolstoy (1828-1910) said, "Wrong does not cease to be wrong because of the majority share in it." Just because a large group of people says something is right, does not make it so. You will find in life, many times the majority is wrong on most things. As Mark Twain said, "Whenever you find yourself on the side of the majority, it is time to pause and reflect."

Most people are all too aware of the controversy that the BSA had when they changed their long standing policy about gays in Scouts. I do not want to get into the rights and wrongs about homosexuality here. It is not my purpose, however, I would like to point out a few facts that I believe are relevant .

First, if anyone thought that up until the time the BSA changed its policy that there were no gays in Scouts, then they are living in a different universe. Of course, there were. Homosexuality is not some new accurence in society. Also, if you think that just by recognizing that there are gays in Scouts will cause some kind of danger to boys, you are mistaken there too. I am not saying that there is no danger for sexual abuse. That is a real danger everywhere. Sexual abuse can happen in school, at gatherings, church, Scouts or even in the home. The problem is not to ban people, but to prepair them.

May I encourage anyone interested to read the program in Scouting called Youth Protection Training. You will find a copy of this in the front of every Scout handbook. It must be read by both the parents and the Scout for them to be part of a troop. Every adult myst take the training class before they can take a role in Scouting. In fact, you cannot be part of a Scout outing without having taken this course. Scouts also always practice two deep leadership. That means that no adult is ever alone with a Scout who is not their child. I honestly do not know of any porganization who does more for the safty of children that the BSA.

The Scout Oath and Law have not changed, all Scouts are to abide by these key principles. No Scout, whether homosexual or heterosexual, is to be sexually active, period. These are children and sexual activity of any kind is prohibited.

One mistake that so many people have is thinking that heterosexual activity is normal for a young man and therefore okay. Sexual activity of any kind is out of bounds for the Scout. No Scout should be encouraged to be sexually active outside of marriage, which between the ages of 11 and 18 years old is not going to happen.

I am also disturbed by the uproar about gay leaders, when nothing is said about leaders who are living with some-one outside of marriage. Is it okay to tell our youth that one form of immorality is better than another? It is also silly to

> "If you make listening and observation your occupation you will gain much more than you can by talk."
> **Sir Robert Baden-Powell**
> **1857-1941**
> **Founder of The Boy Scouts**

think that just because a person is gay they are going to jump every adult, child, or household pet of the same gender. Most gay adults have the same self-control as heterosexual adults who are leaders or teachers. Yes, things have happened that are not acceptable, from both groups. The problem, however, is not their sexual orientation, but their lack of self-discipline.

I am a Christian and I hold to the principles taught in the Word of God about sexual behavior and what is right and what is wrong. Again, my purpose here is not to get into this discussion. It does, however, concern me that people can be so vocal about things that their own lives do not reinforce. You cannot compromise on one thing and be hard on another.

Here is the thing about this whole controversy that bothers me the most, and it has to do with my fellow Christians more than those who do not profess a faith.

Allow me to start by making it clear that the change of position of the BSA toward homosexuality was a disappointment to me. Not so much because it allowed gays into the Scouting program. Like I had said, to think they were not there to start with is silly. And, personally, I believe Scouting is an excellent program for a boy, all boys. What disappointed me was they chose to make an issue that did not have to be one. The leadership, not the Scouts themselves, let outside forces cause them to weaken and compromise on issues of morality and conscience. This I find a breach of what Scouting teaches and stands for.

This compromise also brought into the program something that should not be there and that is the issue of sexual activity. Scouts are clean, that means they are not sexually active in any way. The message given now is it is okay under certain conditions to be sexually active. It needs to be made clear that this is not only not okay, but still, can mean that a Scout can be removed from the program.

My disappointment with fellow Christians is as soon as something happens, they did not like or support, they cut and ran. I see this far too often in the world we live in. Christians will walk away from things that are outside of what we believe is good and right, rather than stay and make a change that is needed. So much of the loss of Christian influence in our society is not because the world is stronger than we are, it is because, rather than make a change, we throw up our hands and take our toys, and run home.

It is because of the changes in programs like the Scouts that Christians should be more involved than ever. How are we to be salt and light to the world when we choose to have nothing to do with? The forces of this world have not won in Scouts, our schools or our government, we surrendered. The blame for the lack of positive influence in this world is ours, not theirs. Remember, Jesus did not come into the world to call the righteous, but sinners to repentance. If we are to see changes for the better, we best decide to be the change.

The whole purpose of adult leaders in the Scouting program is to be an influence and example. We are to be the example of the Scout Oath and Law. We are to be the example of making good and proper decisions. We are to be an example of kindness and understanding. Doesn't it make sense to be the example of good morals and Godly living? How can you be an example of anything if you are not there? To those, you leave behind; you are an example of snobbery and rejection.

As a Christian, I am called to make a difference in this world, not because I am better than they are, but because I too am a sinner. The only difference is that I found the One – the only One – who can forgive my sins and cleanse me from unrighteousness. Actor, Kirt Cameron said it well when he said, "What I would say is Jesus came to save lost sinners like you and me, and if Jesus Christ has a burning desire to seek and save the lost, then you should, too, if Christ is living within you. If you don't have a concern for the lost, then I am concerned about your salvation because the Holy Spirit wants the lost to come to Christ."

It is our responsibility as Christian folks, to influence and bring change to every aspect of our society. If you want to see change for the better, then be that change. Do not abandon those who you disagree with, stay and be the example of what is right. Do not think that starting a Christian version of something is the Godly thing to do. Jesus did not avoid the sinners of His time in order to start a Christian version of things. He ate and drank with sinners and walked and talked with them. He spent His time with them. And here is the key to it all, once He did all that, the sinners were never the same again. He did not cause change He was the change.

Christians who hide from the things of this world are useless to the work of God. The only way you will make a difference is to get in there and be a part of it all. If you are worried about being tarnished by the world, than your faith in Christ is much too flawed. We are all beggars looking for answers. The difference is you can tell other beggars where to find them. I love the words of pastor, and the author of the hymn, Amazing Grace, John Newton (1725-1807) who said, "Although my memory's fading, I remember two things very clearly, I am a great sinner and Christ is a great Savior."

CHAPTER 14

BEING DEVOUT

(A Scout is Reverent)

"Be on alert, stand firm in the faith, act like men, be strong."

St. Paul

1 Corinthians 16:13

"A Scout is reverent. A Scout is reverent toward God. He is
faithful in his religious duties. He respects the beliefs of others."

The Boy Scout Handbook

13ᵗʰ Edition

Every teaching on success will tell you that there is a definite spiritual element of true success. Where I may differ from some is that you will often hear that what you are spiritual about is not as important as just being spiritual about something. I do not believe that because what we give our heart to will have a definite effect on what we do and how we live.

I have also found many who, in not wanting to offend anyone, will dance around their faith and consider it a matter of privacy, but I am not one for that tactic. I am a Christian and my life belongs to Jesus Christ. I also believe that He is truly God, the only means of salvation, and I believe the Bible is the true, flawless word of God.

Now, having said that, I do respect the fact that each of us is entitled to our own beliefs. I may not agree with them, but it is not my place to dictate to you what to believe. The Boy Scouts of America declare this statement; "The Boy Scouts of America believes that you can't grow into the best kind of citizen without recognizing your duty to God. However, Scouting is nonsectarian, which means it doesn't tell members what to believe or how to worship." When it comes to Scouting, I follow this direction. I do not challenge or correct anyone, youth or adult, on their religious beliefs. However, if asked, I will always tell the truth.

It is my place, to be honest, and truthful with you, the reader of this book. I promised to do that at the beginning. If I were to say your beliefs do not matter, I would not be truthful. As I go from here, understand Who I am talking about when I say God, and Who

"We are not a club or a Sunday school class, but a school of the woods."

Sir Roibert Baden-Powell
1857-1941
Founder of The Boy Scouts

I believe is the only source of salvation and power to live a truly success-ful life. In the words of the 19th-century pastor and evangelist Charles Spurgeon, "Morality will keep you out of jail — but only the blood of Jesus will keep you out of Hell."

One of the important things about developing spiritual understanding is we all need to have something greater than ourselves to believe in. After all, if we are all we have, even at our very best, we are a very sorry people. Success-minded people see that they serve a greater power who is good, loving and able to help them in times of need. It is one thing to talk about being good, honorable and a person of real integrity, but it is another to put it into practice. As humans, it takes all the effort we have to live right all the time. We need help. We can find help by developing a relationship with God and by following His word in our lives. I often read these verses from the book of Ecclesiastes 12:13-14, "Now all has been heard; here is the conclusion of the matter: Fear God and keep His commandments, for this is the duty of all mankind. For God will bring every deed into judgment, including every hidden thing, whether it is good or evil."

Duty to God is a very important part of Scouting, Scouts are encouraged, not only to follow the religious practices of their family, but they are also encouraged to serve in some way within their church or place of worship. This service helps the Scout see that religion is not just something for one day a week or to say "I am this faith or that," but it is to hold meaning and importance in their lives.

One of the misunderstandings people have about the Bible and Christian life is that it is a bunch of rules of things you cannot do. You cannot do this and you have to keep away from that and they see it as too restrictive and unreasonable to follow. The fact of the matter is that it is just the opposite. As a Christian, I can do whatever I wish. I have a choice (Christianity, by the way, is one of the only faiths in the world that gives you a choice). I can follow God and His commands, or I can choose not to. Of course, as with all things in life, my choice has its consequences.

I know God loves me and wants the best for me. Therefore, if I follow the way He has given me to live, I will find life and fullness. He wants to give me the best life I can have. It may not be an easy or prosperous life, but it will be the best. If I choose to not follow Him, He also shows me that it, too, has consequences. Most are not what I want in my life and so the choice is mine. I follow Him because I want to; I love Him, not because He gave me no choice, but because it is what I choose. Several years ago my family was vacationing in Ireland and came upon the ruins of an old Abby. In it was the grave of a nun of the late 1700's; the saying on her grave became the message of my life. It read, "I am His, and His I choose to be."

Success-minded people also know that their faith is an anchor when things get rough. And things will get rough. No one has a life that is always smooth and wonderful. We all have difficulties, heartbreaks and disappointments in life. We all have to work and make difficult decisions and hard choices every day. Faith allows us the stability to do all that and more. It is a foundation on which our life is built. When things get shaken, we know the foundation will hold.

Success-minded people and Scouts are not perfect. No one is so put together that they do not suffer at times and make wrong decisions or poor choices. As the French playwright, Moliere said, "Oh, I may be devout, but I am human all the same." Our faith allows us forgiveness, restoration, and strength to move on. No need to be trapped in the bondage of past mistakes, we learn and we move on. That is a life of faith.

HERE FOR A REASON

There are two schools of extreme thought people have when it comes to thinking about who we are. One is that you are the center of the universe and have to think of yourself first. You and your happiness are all that matters and forget the rest of mankind. The other is just as odd, it is that you are a worm; a nothing and you are just here to live till you die. That it is wrong and immoral for you to think of yourself and you must suffer for others in order to have any value in this life at all.

Whether it is a big ego or a sense of worthlessness, the wrong thinking about yourself is damaging to you and to those around you. In Scouting, we strive to see that young men have a healthy and honest view of themselves and of other people. You cannot see the world from a positive light, unless you can first see yourself for who you were created to be. The famous coach, Vince Lombardi (1913-1970) used to say, "Life's battles don't always go to the stronger or faster man. But sooner or later the man who wins is the man who thinks he can."

Here are four things that we need to believe about ourselves in order to be a healthy and productive person.

1) YOU HAVE VALUE

Each and every one of us was put on this planet for a purpose. God (who I believe has created us all) did not have a quota to fill, and you are not just some biological happening. You have a purpose and that purpose is good and

"Vigorous Scout games are the best form of physical education because most of them bring in moral education."
Sir Robert Baden-Powell
1857-1941
Founder of The Boy Scouts

important. You are here to make a difference, which makes you of great value to the rest of the world. Success-minded people not only see this, but also recognize that everyone else was created with a purpose and has great value. Success-minded people respect and encourage that value in themselves and in others.

Scouts know that to be our best, means we make a difference in the world. Why else would you work so hard to be your best? Remember, as already stated, it is to be your best, not be the best. Scouts do not allow ego to get in the way of their success. Take another quick look at the

Scout Oath; it says they are to do their best for God and country, to help others and be an example of the value of the Scout Law. That is a tall order that can only be filled with the help of the One who created them in the first place.

2) GOD GAVE YOU A DREAM

So just what is the purpose you were born for? I believe that is what we call our dream. In each of us, there is something we have always wanted to do or be. It comes to us when we dream, when changes happen in our lives or when we have time to daydream about what we would do if life were perfect. You were meant to achieve that dream, so embrace it and go after it with all that is in you. After all, if the Creator of the universe gave you a dream, how can you fail?

Scouting is still one of the organizations allowing young people to dream and then encourage those dreams. Scouts are not told to be insensible or to keep their feet on the ground. Scouts are allowed to dream of the impossible and can even dream of the impractical. When we are young we see the romance of all the different jobs in life. We want to be a fireman one day and a trash collector the next. Young people often want to do jobs of the people they look up to and respect. The thing is if allowed to dream, those many dreams will form into their true dream, their purpose. Do not tell the young what they should do in life let them find it. After all, it is their dream. I agree with the words of English historian, G.M. Trevelyan (1876-1962) who said, "Never tell a young person that anything cannot be done. God may have been waiting centuries for someone ignorant enough of the impossible to do that very thing."

3) YOU CAN DO THIS

The whole world can believe in you, but it makes little difference until you believe in you. Know that you can achieve your dreams if you are willing to give it all you have, stay with it and make it happen. You have to want the dream in order to make the dream come into reality. Racecar driver, Mario Andretti said, "Desire is the key to motivation, but it's the determination and commitment to the unrelenting pursuit of your goal - a commitment to excellence - that will enable you to attain the success you seek."

When a young person first enters Scouting, the idea of becoming an Eagle is impossible. It is like thinking they are becoming a brain surgeon or something. They see it as a lot of work, commitment, and skill. It does not take long for that wall to break down. Why? Because they begin to believe they can do this. They are told by their leaders that they can achieve the Eagle rank if they desire to. Not, if they study hard, or if they have the skills needed. It is based purely on desire. If you want it you can do it. They see other Scouts who they know are no more talented than they are, but possibly more committed, make Eagle. Soon they know they can have it if they want it...and they want it bad.

4) YOU WERE BORN TO BE GREAT

"You were born to win," said author, Zig Ziglar, "but to be a winner, you must plan to win, prepare to win, and expect to win." Understand that you were not created to be mediocre or to just get by. You were created to make a difference and to do the extraordinary. You have no idea what wonderful things you can do, until you step out and try. Go for the gold in life and never settle for anything but excellence from yourself.

Here is a fact every Scout or success-minded person must know, only ordinary people can do extraordinary things. There really are no extraordinary people in the world, just ordinary people who do extraordinary things. This was not a mistake in creation; it was God's purpose for us to be able to do far more than we believe we are capable of. He always does His best work with inferior materials. He did not create us to be perfect, He did create us to strive for perfection, however.

DUTY TO GOD AND COUNTRY

"I believe with all my heart that standing up for America, means standing up for the God who has blessed our land." Said the 40th President of the United States, Ronald Reagan (1911-2004). "We need God's help to guide our nation through stormy seas. But we can't expect Him to protect America in a crisis if we just leave Him over on the shelf in our day-to-day living." In Scouting there is no separation between Duty to God and Duty to Country, they stand together and are done together.

Just as with Christmas, when people tend to think of religious things like going to church, celebrating the birth of Christ with manger scenes and Bible readings at family gatherings, so we also think of country during the Fourth of July. The Fourth of July is a time we put out our flags, celebrate America with picnics, fireworks, and parades. It also has a religious aspect that we recognize. We are, after all, One Nation Under God. We recognize God on our money, in our pledge and favorite patriotic songs.

What does it mean to be a nation under God? Over the years, the way Americans look at God has changed. God has become more of a symbol than a reality to many. It is nice to call on Him in times of trouble and need, but we do not wish to submit to His laws or standards. No one wants to be "too religious." We will fill churches after a tragedy like 9/11, but to ask for people to live daily devoted to God and the path He calls us to, well, that is asking a bit much.

We have had the same problem in Scouting, we talk of our duty to God and the Scout Spirit, but it is not really stressed or thought of as a key part of Scouting. We have a religious emblem Scouts can earn, but it does not hold the same importance as a merit badge and you do not have to have any in order to become an Eagle. Like much of our society, religion is smiled at, but not seen as a must.

"Scouting is nothing less than applied Christianity."
Sir Robert Baden-Powell
1857-1941
Founder of The Boy Scouts

Too many Americans see the rise in crime, poverty, injustice, and immorality and ask, "Where is God?" When all the time God is saying, "Where are you?" Once a person or group of people, push God out of their daily lives, disaster is sure to follow. Not because God is punishing us, but because we have walked away from His protection. And when that lack of submission to the standards of God and what is right and good happens in our leadership, then we have no option, but to prepare for the worst. As our first President, George Washington (1732-1799) wisely said, "It is impossible to rightly govern a nation without God and the Bible."

Yet, God has always had a people. No matter what the culture or government does, God has always had a people. Though there is a collapse of moral judgment, there is fear of crime and injustice, the presence of terror and pain, God has always had a people. And it is His people, those who have done their best to be faithful to their God, who are the hope for the future of this great land. These people, although far from perfect, are the ones who know that living by God's standards, is the only way to return to a nation under God.

We have come to a crossroad in this country. We can take the path that many will follow. It requires relying on the leadership of the nation to guide us. It is based on each person doing what is right in his or her eyes. Allowing, in the name of caring and unity, people to practice any form of morality they feel is good for them. As eighteenth century Irish statesman, Edmund Burke (1729-1797) said, "The only thing necessary for the triumph of evil is for good people to do nothing."

The other path means that we, who desire to have a better life and follow the ways of God, take a stand and set the pace. The change will not come through new and harder laws, or by forcing people to do what we know is right. Change only happens through a change of heart and when people know the right and better way. It is unreasonable to expect Godly behavior out of unGodly people. If they do not know God, why would we expect them to follow Him? We must set the pace. We were called to be salt and light to this world. We are to be responsible and self-reliant in the midst of irresponsibility and dependence. We are the change makers, but that change, first must be to us, before we can expect it in the world around us.

In the Boy Scout Oath, young people promise to, "Do my duty to God and my Country." They are instructed, not only to know the oath, but understand its meaning as well. To do one's duty is to be willing to do right, no matter the cost. To do your duty is not a group project, but a pledge to be responsible for your own actions and attitudes. As former President, Calvin Coolidge (1872-1933) said, "Duty is not collective; it is personal."

The purpose for a Scout committing to do his duty to God, is the same as it is to follow the Scout Law. It means he will be an example of Godly living and what it means to have God active in his life. It is the same as his following the Scout Law and being the example of all the points in that law. Scouts have a responsibility to be the standard for others to follow, whether they are Scouts or not. The 43rd President, George W. Bush said, "Times and challenges change, yet the values of Scouting will never change. Scouts of any era would recognize every word that you live by today because those words have always defined Scouting. The goodness of a person and of the society he or she lives in, often comes down to very simple things, and the words found in the Scout Law. Every society depends on trust and loyalty, on courtesy and kindness, on bravery and reverence. These are the values of Scouting, and these are the values of America."

I would like for us to look at a few simple, yet profound ways that we can do our duty to both God and our country. These are things that each of us must be personally responsible for as an exhibit in our daily lives. As I said, change must first happen to us before we can see it in the world around us. You have great power in your personal thoughts and behaviors. You may think you do not matter and that you're only one person. However, you do matter and it is in the power of each individual person that we see any change. Look throughout history, all great changes started with only one person. That might as well be you.

BE WILLING TO LIVE AS AN EXAMPLE

People are watching you; those around you watch to see how you live and what you do. Does your walk match your talk? Do you believe the things you say? Do not be deceived into thinking that no one notices you. We live in a time where true privacy is very small. Social media, technology and the ability to spy on others, has made it hard to be private about anything. The good news is, as people can see when we goof up or do the wrong thing, they can see when we do the right thing too.

As a Christian, we are called to be public in all we do. You are to be the example to others in how to act and think. In the Scripture verse, 1 Timothy 4:12 we are told, "...but rather in speech, conduct, love, faith, and purity, show yourself an example of those who believe." What you say, whether positive and encouraging words or negative and destructive words, it matters. How you behave, whether being kind, pleasant, polite and helpful or mean, rude, uncaring and judgmental, it matters. Whether you show love, faithfulness, trustworthiness or hate, cruelty and dishonesty, it matters. If you show your faith and trust in Christ in all things and are not ashamed to be named among His followers or if you are a fair weather Christian, who goes to church on Sunday and lives in the world the other six days of the week, it matters. If you know how to keep yourself clean and pure, not giving into sex outside of marriage, pornography or perverted living, it matters.

Why does it matter? Because people need to know that it is possible to live for God and still be a happy person. The general public is taught that Christians are unhappy, restricted and unkind, but just the opposite is true. We are the freest, most loving and positive people on the planet.

I follow Christ because I choose to, not because I have to. I give Him my love and loyalty freely; He does not take it from me. But If I do not show that to those around me, how will they know that He is for real?

Of course, we know that the Apostle Paul's young padawan, Timothy, was not a Scout. There were no Scouts in the first-century church. However, I bet he would have been one if there were. Timothy is a young man who took on the big, impossible role of a pastor to the church of Ephesus. Being young, I am sure he faced many of the challenges that young people do today.

It is a myth that people were different in past times. Yes, the culture was different, social structure was different as were customs, lifestyle, and fashion. What was not different were people. They laughed and cried as we do today and they had the same needs we do today. People loved, fought, followed God and served each other as we do today. Once we start to see that the nature of people, were the same as today, we start to understand them and why they did the things they did.

Scouting may not have been around in the first-century, but the desire to be a good and Godly person was. The very principles that make up the Scout Law were in effect then as they are now. There was still a need to be

> "O God, help me to win, but in thy wisdom if thou willest me not to win, then O God, make me a good loser."
> **Sir Robert Baden-Powell**
> **1857-1941**
> **Founder of The Boy Scouts**

trustworthy, loyal, helpful, friendly, courteous, kind, obedient, cheerful, thrifty, brave, clean and reverent. The life and behavior of a young man was very important, just as it is today.

Be a person who is positive, caring and grateful. That will speak more to the world around you than anything you say. As Saint Francis of Assisi said, "Preach the gospel at all times, when necessary, use words." You are the gospel to those around you and your attitude and actions will bring great change.

BE WILLING TO STAND FOR WHAT IS RIGHT

We are constantly being fed the idea that compromise is the best thing people can do. When you do not agree on something, then there should be a compromise. That is a lie from the pit of hell, for one thing, those who demand compromise; define it as agreeing with them. There is no meeting in the middle. You see this in government all the time. One side cries for compromise, compromise, and yet, when it comes down to it, what they want is their own way. This has never worked, and will never work. As former British Prime Minister, Lady Margaret Thatcher (1925-2013) said, "If you just set out to be liked, you would be prepared to compromise on anything at any time, and you would achieve nothing."

We have talked about this earlier, so I will not repeat what I have already said. I do want to stress that when we talk about not compromising, we are not saying you never change your mind or direction. Sometimes in life, you will find that other people have discovered a better way of doing things. Some times their ideas are as good, or better, than yours. In these cases, you may wish to compromise and agree or a mixture of the two. However, if this compromise involves lowering your standards and doing what you know to be wrong, then you do not compromise at all. No compromise includes anything unethical, immoral or illegal.

The point to remember is there are absolutes in life. There are absolute truth and absolute lies; there is no middle ground. Something cannot be partly true or your truth and my truth. Things are true or they are not. God is truth and that is all there is to it, He is not true because I or anyone else believes it. He is truth whether everyone in the world does not believe it. He is the truth and His word (the Bible) is the truth. There is no argument about if you believe that or not or if I believe that or not. There is no compromise about the Bible being a "good book." There is no what about other religious books or whether some people in the deepest jungles have not seen a Bible. God is true and allows every man be a liar.

Standing for truth means we do not back down when confronted or disagreed with. It means standing alone sometimes, it means that some may call you names, put you in prison or harm you. Standing for truth is never being willing to compromise what you know is right.

BEING WILLING TO DO SOMETHING

What can you do? How about running for office? That is right, what we need is to have more and more good people in places of leadership. The world has not taken over our culture, but rather we have surrendered it. Over the past 100 years or so, Christians have hidden in their churches, had their own groups and kept away from what they saw as "the secular world." What has happened was the influence that the church was to have in the world, has diminished into almost nothing.

Author, C.S. Lewis (1898-1963) once said, "We do not need any more books about Christianity. What we need is more books on other subjects written by Christians." That goes for all areas of life. We must, once again, be the influence that sets the path for the world we live in. Christianity is not just how we practice our religion, it is how we live life, do business, art, and education. There is no aspect of our human life that it does not touch. It is not a religious view it is a worldly view. There will always be those who are unGodly and corrupt. There is no getting away from that. However, we do not have to allow them to run the world.

The same principle applies to Scouts, if you want to make a difference, do something. Throughout the history of Scouting, you will find humble Scouts who went on to do great things and influence the world they live in. This book has had many stories about the ways Scouts have influenced others. Just as we need more Christians involved in government, organizations and the marketplace, so we need those who live by the principles of the Scout Law.

There is another way to influence the world and many people can do it. May I be an example to you with this book? You got it. It is to write.

Writing, whether a book, an article or a blog, you can reach many people all at the same time. The great reformer, Martin Luther (1483-1586) said, "If you want to change the world, pick up your pen and write." There are many people out there who have something to say, and this could be the best way to say it.

It does get tiring to hear Christian people who fuss and complain about the government and yet, do not do anything to change it. Pastor and religious leader, Jerry Falwell (1933-2007) rightly said, "The idea that religion and politics don't mix was invented by the Devil to keep Christians from running their own country." It is time we start stepping up to the challenge of leadership in politics, education, business, medicine and all areas of life.

We have a duty to both God and country to be the best we can be and be responsible for our nation. Conservative political activist, Alan Keyes said, "Our first responsibility is not to ourselves. Our first responsibility is to our country and to our God." We have a duty to be a catalyst of change to the culture we live in and live in a way that will make things better for all. To succeed in all we do with excellence so that we have set a new standard for the world to follow. God's standard.

BEING A FANATIC

I have been called a fanatic about many things. I confess, the accusation is true...I am a fanatic. I am a fanatic about the principles of Scouting because I think it is good for a person to possess the character described in the

"In Scouting, a boy is encouraged to educate himself instead of being instructed."
**Sir Robert Baden-Powell
1857-1941
Founder of The Boy Scouts**

Scout Law. I am a fanatic about good manners. I believe recapturing good manners will improve and transform our society. I am a fanatic about my Christian Faith. I believe there is nothing better than to know the only one God through His Son, Jesus Christ. Yes, I am a fanatic!

Let's look at the principles that are in the Scout Law. For a person to work at being trustworthy, loyal, helpful, friendly, courteous, kind, obedient, cheerful, thrifty, brave, clean and reverent is a wonderful thing. What can you honestly find wrong in that list of qualities? As the novelist, John Irving stated, "Good habits are worth being fanatical about."

I know there will be someone out there who feels that asking someone to be a person of character, is asking too much, but then we have always had to give way to fools. Who can be against someone being kind or honest or giving or cheerful? There are no down sides to this. I see the same in those who have good manners. What can be wrong with a person treating others with respect and grace?

We live in a time when some think that being a fanatic is a bad thing. If you are a fanatic toward bad behavior or habits, then it is wrong. Common sense, which we all know is not so common anymore, tells us the difference between right and wrong. You do not need laws or rules to tell you what decent and good behavior is.

Success-minded people do their best to live daily in what is right and good. They know that bad habits and bad behavior bring destruction and hurt. There is no success when dishonesty and injustice are in play. Because of this, success-minded people work hard at being the best they can be. They enrich the lives of those who are around them and they stand for what is right.

There are times when standing for what is right and living your life by good principles, is a lonely road. However, if the only person who I must answer to is my God, then I will always want to be honorable and know that I am doing my best.

SCOUTS AND INTERFAITH

We have already made it clear that the Boy Scouts of American is a nonsectarian organization and do not hold to one religious view. That is a good thing. I know that with stating my Christian views as clearly as I have, you would think I would insist that the BSA was a Christian organization. However, The Boy Scouts of America is an organization that focuses on the character and personal development of young people.

There are many groups all over the world that desire to help develop people, young and old, into good citizens and better people. Each may have a faith component, but they are not a religious organization. I believe one of the problems people have had with Scouts is that they mistakenly believed it was religious and was not living up to its faith systems. Being reverent, the 12th point of the Scout Law is a mark of character, not the endorsement of any religious belief.

The Scout Law states that a Scout should show respect toward God, do their duty and be faithful to their religious beliefs, and have respect for the beliefs of others, who may differ from your own. All these are good points of character that should be practiced by all people.

I have told you that I hold fast to my Christian faith and do not compromise it in any way. However, I also said that I could respect the beliefs of others who do not hold to my faith. Note, I said I respect other beliefs, I did not say I believed them to be true or that I practice them in any way. I simply believe we all have the choice to believe as we wish and it is not up to me to dictate what others' faith should be. It is the same for those who hold no faith at all. Do I believe they are right and they will meet God in their own way? No. I believe there is only one way to God, however, if people wish to look else where I cannot stop them from doing so. I will be honest when asked what I believe to be true, but I cannot force anyone to believe anything.

Here is where I differ from the BSA policy on religion. The BSA has strived to have what they call an interfaith system. This is where all faiths can function together at the same time. Kind of like saying they are all true and therefore, you can practice any or all belief systems. The truth is, they are not all the same, nor do they all follow the same denomination of God, and the different faiths themselves do not believe this. Each will tell you they are the true faith.

I have sat on religious programming committees and seen Scout leaders struggle to figure out how to get all different groups...Christian, Muslim, Jewish, Buddhists etc...together for a worship service or activity that blends them together. They have such things, but tend to be poorly attended and cause more problems than they should.

Here is what I believe is how the BSA should handle the 12th point of the Scout Law, just leave it alone. The Law is clear, "A Scout is reverent toward God. He is faithful in his religious duties. He respects the beliefs of others." That is not only clear, it is good. As with the other points of the Scout Law, it is up to the Scout to fulfill the law in their life.

I see the BSA encouraging the Scouts to see God and learn about his duty to God and his religious beliefs. The religious emblem, for instance, is a very good tool to help Scouts follow their faith. The material used for this is designed for the different faiths it serves. It is not one book or class that covers them all. They are designed to help the Scouts better understand their own religions.

The question is why do they try to force these same Scouts, who are learning their own faith, to believe in or practice in some way, other faiths? The standard to earn the emblem is in place, so leave it alone. Allow the Scout to earn it and follow the direction of his family and their religious leaders.

"It is not the slightest use to preach the Scout Law or to give it out as orders to a crowd of boys: each mind requires its special exposition of them and the ambition to carry them out."

Sir Robert Baden-Powell
1857-1941
Founder of The Boy Scouts

Learning of them or taking part in them in any way does not show respect for other faiths. I can respect the fact there are Muslim believers (just one example) in Scouting. I can respect the fact they do not believe as I do, and their worship will be different than mine. However, I do not wish to take part in their prayer time because we are praying to different gods, and I do not pray to any God, but the one I know to be true. I do not need to follow, know or serve any other religion, but my own. By serving my own beliefs, I am fulfilling the 12th point of the Scout Law, doing my duty to God and am a better person for it.

The same is true looking at this from other faiths. A Muslim believer is not going to want to be a part of my teachings on following Jesus, not as a Buddhist or Christianity or Islam. Why do we try to make them? I believe we should allow each Scout to fill this point as their faith and heart dictate.

The same is true at camps; I believe it is a good thing for Scouts to have a worship service at camp. But why call on a Christian Chaplain to include a Jewish or Islamic prayer in his service? This applies to any mix of faiths. Allow each to hold their own service in the way they believe will strengthen the faith of the Scouts they serve.

I understand this can be a sticky point for the BSA as a whole. However, it need not be. As I said, the BSA is not a religious organization. Many religious organizations, like churches, are Troop charter partners. These charter partners believe in Scouting and support the Scout Law, however, they see their Troop as an outreach of their church and that is why they do not go to interfaith services. They will hold a Scout service on Scout Sunday, (always in February) but they do not wish to explore other faiths.

I support the principles taught in the Scout Law, including the 12th point, however, I do believe the Scout should be able to fulfill that point, earn religious emblems and follow his faith without having to be involved in others. Respect them, yes. Never attack or say or do anything that belittles or opposes any other faith. Scouts respect the freedom of religious beliefs as they do all freedoms we hold dear, but their practice and services are to their own beliefs at all times.

And so it is with the success-minded person, we should always be growing and developing in our faith. It is never enough, even for adults, to just go to church now and then. You need to seek out God in your life and serve Him at all times. I am not saying you grab your Bible and evangelize the workplace. I am saying that as believers in Christ, there is no part of our lives that He does not touch or that He does not belong.

The successful Christian should have daily time with God by reading the Bible, applying the lessons gained there and in prayer. Prayer for direction when making decisions and prayer for needs of ourselves and others. Prayer for help to be the best you can be. God is not a part of our lives, He is our living, breathing lives. Our relationship with God needs to be the most important thing you do. There is no real success without Him. Not even close.

CHAPTER 15

CONCLUSION

"The aim of The Boy Scouts is to supplement the various existing educational agencies, and to promote the ability in boys to do things for themselves and others."

The Boy Scout Handbook

1911

My hope and prayer is that this book in some way was a benefit to you as you have spent the time to read it. As you know, I respect the time and do not take the use of it, especially if I am the one taking it from you. I do know that if you have read this far you have a desire to improve as a person and discover the great things you were created to do.

My desire for writing this book is found in three things. First, I wanted to write a book based on the Scout Oath and Law that Scouts could use as they grow into adulthood. While in Scouts, they will hear these principles over and over again. They will see them posted on the trails and in the dining pavilions at camp. They will recite them at every meeting and event. They are an important part of the life of a Scout. However, once they become an adult, they find they have to look for these in order to see them. They are not on the wall in their workplace, unless you get a job with the BSA. They no longer recite them with their friends at a weekly meeting. At this point in life, the Scout Oath and Law must be part of who they are and in turn, it will affect what they do.

I tried to show how these principles apply to the life of a success-minded person in the everyday world. No matter if you are involved in Scouting still or have moved on to other activities, the Scout Oath and Law will be your guide to success in all areas of life.

Second, This is for those who have known Scouting, yet have not seen how it can work in your life today. Maybe you were a Scout in your younger years, perhaps you know a Scout, a friend or your own children. Or maybe you have just liked what Scouting seemed to stand for, but thought it was for someone else and not you. I pray you will see that Scouting was for you then and it still is today.

You do not have to be an active Scout for the principles in the Scout Law to work in your life. As said before, these principles work because they are real and true, not because you choose to believe in them. You can be a Scout, a former Scout, (although any Scout will tell you that there is no such thing as a former Scout. Once a Scout, always a Scout.)

Or you've never dealt with Scouting at all and these 12 points of the Scout Law will make your life better, more successful and help you achieve the impossible.

Lastly, this book was for anyone who seeks to be his or her best and live a life worth living. We have talked much about the success-minded person in this book. That is because it takes the wisdom, determination, and courage of a success-minded person to follow the principles of the Scout Oath and Law. I am well aware that some will see this book and think they are more advanced in knowledge than this. "Scouting is for kids, not an intelligent and savvy person like me."

If you are too smart to be bothered with the simple and common sense teachings of the Scout Oath and Law, you will never grow and become all you were created to be. We all need to understand that we have much to learn as people. Also, the greatest and most profound truths in life are often the simplest. Reality is, it is because the truth is often simple and open for anyone, that most people miss it.

Look at God's plan for the salvation of humankind. In the gospel of John, chapter 3 verse 16 it simply states, "For God so loved the world that He gave His only Son, that whosoever believes in Him may not perish but have everlasting life." You cannot get more simple and clear than that, and yet, more people in this world have missed it, then got it. Never make the mistake of thinking that because something is not complicated or difficult to understand that it is not important. Truth is always simple and easy to understand for those who are willing to learn, grow and change.

In writing this book, I too have found many new and wonderful discoveries that have bettered my life. Not because I am such a great writer and thinker (I am under no illusions), but because I am open to learning. I have done much research and taken time to think through the things I am saying here and therefore, I have learned, just as I hope you have learned, what these principles mean to me and the world I live in.

I do not believe it is possible for a writer to write anything without learning from what he/she has written. It is like being a teacher because any good teacher learns each time they prepare or give a lesson. For the success-minded person, learning is something they could not stop, even if they wanted to – which they don't. When you are open to learning more, discover more and accept that you, in fact, have much to learn, then those lessons can come from anywhere, even from you.

Earlier in this book I talked about all the sources we can learn from; books, other people, mentors and coaches, teachers and so on. One I did not mention was yourself. You will find that if you accept your limited knowledge on anything, you will be open to learning more. As you learn, you think and evaluate what you have learned. That evaluation leads to your own discoveries and you end up teaching yourself things you did not know before. The human mind is an amazing thing, there are no limits to what it can do for the person who is willing to let it loose.

In my blog and articles, I always end with the five elements of personal freedom. These five things, when activated in a personal life, will bring freedom, success, change, and growth. They are to be your best, love God, have good manners, discover the unknown and change your world. Let's look at each of them and see how we can release them in our own lives and really make a difference.

BE YOUR BEST

The well-known Pastor and Author, A.W, Tozer (1897-1963) told us, "Refuse to be average. Let your heart soar as high as it will." That is the key lesson to having a successful life. We talked often in this book about being your best. It is part of the Scout Promise and the encouragement every Scout receives in his Scouting journey, but being you is a bit more than just doing your best.

I have heard people told to "just do your best" like excellence was not expected. Many times adults are guilty of not expecting the best from young people. To them, doing your best means they only need to get by. It is accepting the grade of a C, rather than an A because an A is too hard. News flash, an A is supposed to be hard. That is why it is an A.

I know, to some, this seems hard and uncaring; that is far from true. It is because we care that we should expect the best from our young people. Yes, not all young people will get an A in every thing they do, but they can try. It is a fact of human nature that if given a way out of something, we will take it. Young or old, we always look for the easiest path.

When we are expected to be our best, then we will give our best. No one finds satisfaction in being mediocre. No one likes just getting by. When we are willing to give our best to all we do, we find we are a lot better than we think. Our best then becomes something worth doing and motivates us to be even better next time. Why? Because we now know we can.

Dr. John Maxwell points out that "nobody buys mediocre." We never think about where to go to dinner and say to our spouse, "Let's go to the so and so restaurant. I hear the food there is pretty mediocre." We do not come home from the movies and say, "I loved that film. It was the most mediocre movie I have ever seen." The truth is we do not go back to the mediocre restaurant or see the mediocre movie. Mediocrity is tasteless and void of any excitement or adventure. As human beings, we are repelled by the mediocre life.

Chaplain to King Charles II of England, Thomas Fuller (1608-1661), put it this way, "The real difference between men is energy. A strong will, a settled purpose, and invincible determination can accomplish almost anything and in this lies the distinction between great men and little men." Success-minded people understand the keys to finding your best, lies in your willingness to do the hard work it takes to get there. There is no easy road to excellence and anyone who tells you otherwise is lying to you.

One of the results of a culture that is based on "fairness" and entitlement is that it becomes lazy and unwilling to put forth anymore effort than necessary to get by. There is no incentive to achieve anything great. No one is pushing you forward, but rather telling you to take it easy. But for some, the success-minded among us, greatness is in their nature. They will never settle for second or sit back and be taken care of, these success-minded people are the winners of life.

LOVE GOD

We just covered the 12th point in the Scout Law, A Scout is Reverent. We know that doing our duty to God and practicing our religion is important to who we are as Scouts. The thing is, there is a greater purpose to this than looking at a group, whether Scouts or success-minded people, misses. That is your own personal relationship with God.

Loving God is more than reading your Bible and praying every day. It is not how often you go to church or what ministries you are actively involved in. It is also not found in how much you give of your money, time and skill. A relationship with God is all based on how much you love Him. That love will, in turn, affect every other area of your life. It is in how we live and who we are as a person. As former special counsel to President Richard Nixon and author, Chuck Colson (1931-2012) said, "Loving God – really loving Him – means living out His commands no matter what the cost."

Note, I did not say how much God loves you, but rather how much you love God. That is because He loves you totally and completely, right now, just as you are. He cannot love you more and will not love you less. His love for you is not based on whether you believe in Him or not, He still loves you. It is not based on what you do for Him or not do. You can never earn His love because it is a gift. It is not based on how religious you are, what church or belief system you belong to or how nice you are to others. God loves us all. His love is never the question. Yours is.

God is a loving God, but He is also a just God and He cannot and will not accept sin. Just as He longs to be with us, sin keeps us from Him. We are all, yes, every single one of us, are sinners and will always fall short of what God requires for us to be with Him. So what do we do? Are we lost forever?

God, in His love, made the way for us to receive the forgiveness needed to have that loving relationship with Him. He was willing to send His own perfect Son, Jesus Christ, to the cross to pay for our sins. It is through Him and only Him that we can have a relationship with God and find salvation.

Loving God is loving His Son and when we love His Son, Jesus, we follow Him and live as He has directed us to live. The choice is always ours to make because God's love is never forced on us. Salvation is a gift and as with all gifts, it must be received by us to be ours. You must take it from here.

HAVE GOOD MANNERS

If you were to boil down success in one word, it would have to be others. Often when we think of being successful and achieving success, we think inwardly. It is how we perform, what we achieve and the hard work we put into it. All that is true, but in doing all those things we must always be aware of others and how we affect their lives. How we treat them and what do they gain from our hard work. I am not talking giving things away or charity work, I am talking about how we treat those around us.

Seventeenth century Quaker and the first governor of Pennsylvania, William Penn (1644-1718) put it this way, "I expect to pass through this world but once. Any good therefore that I can do, or any kindness that I can show to any fellow creature, let me do it now. Let me not defer or neglect it, for I shall not pass this way again." William Penn was well aware that if he (or we) is to make a difference in this world and make it better, we have got to show kindness and respect towards others. More importantly, we have to do so now.

Just as the 5th point of the Scout Law tells the Scout to be courteous, good manners are a key to all successful living. Good manners do not just affect how we treat each other, but how others treat us. Good manners, as we have discussed earlier, bring civility into our work, government and church life. Good manners can build a community up or tear it down.

Good manners are needed if you are to achieve your goals in life. The success of any business venture is found in the ability to show good manners. American writer, Letitia Baldrige (1926-2012) said, "Good manners are cost effective. They not only increase the quality of life in the workplace, they contribute to employee morale, embellish the company image, and play a major role in generating profit." There really is no area of life that good manners will not improve and strengthen.

When I talk with people about the qualities of a success-minded person, they are always a bit surprised to find manners on my list. Not that they think manners are unimportant, but they just assume people know that. Besides, how often do you hear a teaching on manners? Yet, good manners are the key to success in our world. Without them, you are just another uncaring person in a sea of uncaring people. With them, you stand out as someone who cares and can be trusted. Or as English author, Quentin Crisp (1908-1999) said, "Manners are love in a cool climate."

To define manners is easy, good manners are nothing more than caring and respecting other people. It is in realizing other people matter and have value. It is the Golden Rule; do to others, as you want them to do to you. That is it. It is not about how you behave at the dinner table or in public gatherings. It has nothing to do with how you use your napkin or sit in a professional meeting. It is all about others. The late Emily Post (1872-1960) who was considered the expert on etiquette said, "Manners are a sensitive awareness of the feelings of others. If you have that awareness, you have good manners, no matter which fork you use."

DISCOVER THE UNKNOWN

One of the most exciting adventures in life is that which is unknown. It is amazing how many people just blindly accept the idea that if it has not been done before, it cannot be done now. Especially in today's climate of living, with what was always impossible. You would think we would know that anything is possible, however, the majority of people do not pursue their dreams because they just assume everything that can be invented has been invented. The Hungarian scientist, Albert Szent-Gyorgyi (1893-1986) tells us, "Discovery consists of seeing what everybody has seen and thinking what nobody has thought."

Do not make the mistake of thinking the so-called experts have all the answers either. What would the world be like if we listened to the experts?

"Everyone acquainted with the subject will recognize it as a conspicuous failure."

- Henry Morton, president of the Stevens Institute of Technology, on the electric light, 1880

"Fooling around with alternating current is just a waste of time. Nobody will use it, ever."

- Thomas Edison, on A/C Current, 1889

"Remote shopping, while entirely feasible, will flop - because women like to get out of the house, like to handle merchandise, like to be able to change their minds."

- Time Magazine, on online shopping, 1966

"While theoretically and technically television may be feasible, commercially and financially it is an impossibility, a development of which we need waste little time dreaming."

- Lee DeForest, American radio pioneer, and inventor of the vacuum tube on television, 1926

"This 'telephone' has too many shortcomings to be seriously considered as a practical form of communication. The device is of no value to us."

- Western Union internal memo on the telephone, 1878

"I think there is a world market for maybe five computers."

- Thomas Watson, chairman of IBM on use of computers, 1943

"We don't like their sound, and guitar music is on the way out."

- Decca Records rejecting the Beatles, 1962

"We have reached the limits of what is possible with computers."

- John Von Neumann, mathematician on the use of computers, 1949

The list can go on and on about what was said, then cannot be done, many times by the very people who invented the product. This we do know, there are a wealth of new discoveries in the world just waiting for those who have the courage and determination to find them. Scientist William Harvey (1578-1657) said, "All we know is still infinitely less than all that remains unknown." We may not hear of all the discoveries made every day, but they are out there. Just look at what has come about in your own lifetime (no matter how old or young you may be). It is amazing to those success-minded people who take the time to look. The sad thing is, so many people go through life and never notice.

So if there are discoveries being made every day by people just like you and me, why can't they be made by you or me? That's right, you could be the one to make the next great discovery that will change the world as we know it. Why not? "But I don't even know where to start," you may say. Listen to the words of author Marcel Proust (1871-1922), "The only real voyage of discovery consists not in seeing new landscapes, but in having new eyes." See things like no one else sees them. Be creative, imaginative and daring. Do not follow what everyone else tells you can be done, follow what you believe can be done. Albert Einstein (1879-1955) said, "Few are those who see with their own eyes and feel with their own hearts." Those few are success-minded people.

The key to new discoveries is curiosity. When we are children we are curious about everything, even a baby is fascinated when he/she discovers his/her hands or feet. I love it when my children and now grandchildren, begin to discover the world they live in. This is a great opportunity to help them learn that the world they see is so much smaller than the world they still have to discover. Curiosity allows us to discover through our senses of touch, hearing, sight, and taste. We begin to ask questions and imagine new and different ways to experience life.

Scouting is all about curiosity and making the discovery. Each camping trip, work is done on merit badges and Scouting activities are a path to discovery. Scouts are not just encouraged to do things they never did before, but they are encouraged to ask questions about everything. Of course, asking questions is just a part of it; the real fun comes in finding the answers. It is when we seek the answers to the questions we have about life, nature, the universe or God that discoveries are made. The better the question, the more powerful the discovery.

Curiosity is the best education in the world. Many of the great educators of our day have discovered that our formal education system, in fact, holds back learning, and does not promote it. Albert Einstein, without question one of the greatest minds of the twentieth century, said, "It is a miracle that curiosity survives formal education." The reason for this is that our education system is designed to give people (children and adults alike) the answers, rather than have them discover them. You are tested and passed on what you have learned, not what you have discovered. In fact, many times curiosity is discouraged because it interrupts the flow of the education system.

I believe in a good education, I am not saying we need to close down schools or that teachers are bad. Teachers, after all, are victims of the same system. They are told what to teach and how to teach it. In many school districts, (I have many friends who are educators who fight this problem) teachers are given the lessons and they are not allowed to deviate from them. Even when they know what they are teaching is wrong.

No great discovery was made due to formal education, it is the curious mind that imagines what cannot be done and how to do it. It is the person who looks where no one else is looking, sees what no one is seeing and questions what no one else is questioning that discovers the unknown. This process must start in the young. God has given the young a curious mind by nature. We cannot stop it and we must encourage it. We need to remember the words of Oliver Wendell Holmes (1841-1935) former Justice on the Supreme Court, who said, "A mind that is stretched by a new experience can never go back to its old dimensions."

One of the unintended weapons that destroy curiosity in children are adults feeling like they always have to answer the questions. We feel that it is our job to be the answer person, rather than to help our children think through the questions they have. Artist, Dave Sutherland said, "Sometimes the questions you ask are more important than the answers you receive." Success-minded people are people who never leave the questioning stage of life. They still need to know "why" to everything.

The whole matter of questions is a wonderful study and far too involved for me to completely cover it. I will say that asking the right questions, quality questions are the pathway to discovery. The people who ask, "Why hasn't someone found an answer to this problem?" will never find the answer to the problem. Why? Because what they are asking is not a quality question that helps them. They are only looking at what is not done. A better question is to ask, "How can I solve this problem?" This begins the thought process that leads to finding answers, not to find reasons.

I love when Scouts come up with better ideas or different ideas to do things. I have often heard a Scout ask,"why do we do it this way?" My response is, "how do you think it should be done?" That is all it takes many times to get the old thinking machine going. In no time at all, they will come up with some different ideas. We allow them to try their ideas to see if they work. Some do, some do not. The important thing is they are learning the process of looking for a better way. This process is what ignites curiosity in a Scout and it never goes away.

CHANGE YOUR WORLD

Of all the challenges that Success-Minded People face, improving the world is the hardest to grasp. I mean think about it...this is the world we are talking about. How can one person make a difference in the lives of billions on this planet? Do I honestly matter in the large scheme of things in this world? I may matter to my family, my business, my church or my circle of friends, but I can't matter to the world. It is just too big and I am far too small.

Now think about this, at every major change in the world since recorded history, how many of them can be traced back to one person. You're right, all of them. It may have been through an idea, an invention, a change in philosophy, or even a political change, but you will find someone, a real human being, who started it off.

I believe someday there will be a cure for cancer or Alzheimers. I believe one day there will be a way to create clean water from polluted water. I believe there will be leaders in the future that will do great things for all people. These are all changes and events that really are not so hard to see. Great things have happened before and greater things are to come. Here is the part that is hard to believe, the person who is making these changes could be you.

When I am working with Scouts, I often wonder what these young people will do in life and what they will achieve. The fact is, we just do not know. People you know and love could be the change agent that the world has been waiting for. It could be your son or daughter, your friend or neighbor, even the person you see in the mirror every morning.

I figure that if I have no idea what the people I come in contact will do, why not treat everyone of them like they had the cure for cancer in their head? Why not encourage every person to do his or her best like the world depended on it? After all, it just might. Isn't it better to think and expect extraordinary things from people, than to think of them as just one in a crowd? We need to think like the young girl who's diary did change the world in her own way, Anne Frank (1925-1945) who said, "How wonderful it is that nobody need wait a single moment before starting to improve the world."

If you study history at all, you know that every time there have been great changes in governments or political movements, it all boils down to one person. Sure others are a part, no one can succeed by themselves, but there is a leader – someone in the front saying, "Come on everyone. Go this way." Look into the achievements in science, medicine, war, exploration, and invention and on and on and you will find someone who had the vision, who led the way, who did the impossible. They all had something in common with the thinking of the great British wartime Prime Minister, Sir Winston Churchill (1874-1965) who said, "Success is not final, failure is not fatal, it is the courage to continue that counts."

When we tell Scouts they are to be brave, we do not just mean to have the courage to do things they never did before or face dangers that may be on the road of life. It takes courage to pursue your dreams. It takes courage to attempt to do what has never been done before. It takes courage to launch out into the unknown and make new and wonderful discoveries. It takes courage to change the world.

Success-Minded People need to understand that you will either improve the world or you will drag it down. There is no standing still – ever! It is contrary to the laws of nature. Even the dead decompose and change the soil. So, if you are going to cause change anyway, why not make it for the better? If someone is going to make a difference, why shouldn't that someone be you?

Just as in the story of Esther who found herself in the middle of a difficult situation. She felt she was no one of importance, but suddenly found she may be able to save her people. Her Uncle Mordecai told her, "And who knows whether you have not attained royalty for such a time as this?" Esther 4:14 God has placed you here for a reason and that reason was not to fill a space. He had intended all along that you would make a difference and improve the world for the better. He is a good God and is always looking out for our best. It was for the betterment of others that God in His love created you. And besides, if the Creator of the universe intended you to do something, how can you fail?

Philosopher Robert M. Pirsig (1928-2017) said, "The place to improve the world is first in one's own heart, head and hands." You start with the one thing you have control of – you! Be the best you that you can be. Be a success-minded person who has integrity, loyalty, is kind and generous. Be a person who can be depended on and trusted at all times. Allow yourself to be creative and adventurous, reaching for the impossible with a heart that believes (as Zig Ziglar always says) that "You can have anything in life that you want as long as you help enough people get what they want." All this and more are in you right now, you only have to draw it out.

"Why push against the stream, when the stream, after all, is running in the right direction."

Sir Robert Baden-Powell

1857-1941

Founder of The Boy Scouts

CPSIA information can be obtained
at www.ICGtesting.com
Printed in the USA
FFOW04n0421020518
46423252-48251FF